LOUISE NEVELSON
29 SPRING STREET
NEW YORK 10012

This is not an
autobiography

This is not a
biography

This is a gift.

L. N.

DAWNS+DUSKS

DAWNS
+
DUSKS

Louise Nevelson

taped conversations
with
Diana MacKown

Charles Scribner's Sons   New York

Library of Congress Cataloging in Publication Data

Nevelson, Louise, 1900–
  Dawns and dusks.

  1. Nevelson, Louise, 1900– 2. Sculptors—
United States—Correspondence, reminiscences, etc.
I. MacKown, Diana. II. Title.
NB237.N43A23   730'.92'4 [B] 76–20634
ISBN 0–684–14781–5

1 3 5 7 9 11 13 15 17 19 M/C 20 18 16 14 12 10 8 6 4 2

Printed in the United States of America

Introduction

$\mathcal{A}$nyone lucky enough to know Louise Nevelson will recognize this book as the next best thing to listening to her talk. Word-by-word transcriptions of recorded conversations seldom relay the true character of the speaker; the rhythms and emphases that differentiate one person's way of talking from another's just don't come through. But Louise Nevelson is present in every phrase of this combination of personal history, philosophical autobiography, and declaration of aesthetic principles by a woman who can be a shrewd observer of the way of the world in one breath and a mystic in the next, without any hiatus or contradiction between the two. Whatever Diana MacKown has done in punctuating and editing the tapes of her conversations with Louise to turn them into a monologue has been just right.

Some years ago when the MacDowell Colony was giving her its annual award, I was asked, as art critic of the *New York Times*, to introduce Louise Nevelson to the audience—a pleasant task in view of my admiration for her work, although I didn't yet know her very well as a person. When she took the podium, where most people would have begun with a modest disclaimer or two, Louise referred to my rapturous introduction and said, "I'll buy that." With the audience in the palm of her hand she went on to tell how good it was to be where she was after years—decades—of working with very little recognition.

During the question period that followed, one woman asked Louise if she would have felt that her life had been well spent—if she would have felt sufficiently rewarded for a life in art—if the recognition had never come; as the questioner put it, "if it had turned out that after all you weren't first-rate." Louise paused for a moment, puzzled (not typical of her). Other artists of the kind called "dedicated" would have answered, "It would still have been worthwhile," which I suspect is what the questioner wanted to hear. But Louise finally said, "It never occurred to me to be anything else." She wasn't fielding the question; she was only stating a simple truth that eliminated it.

This book opens with her elaboration of that point. By the eighth line she is saying, "So I have that blessing, and there was never a time that I questioned or doubted it."

I want everyone to love this book, and I hardly see how anyone who reads it can fail to. Certain passages are so filled with a confidence of inborn powers that they would sound egomaniacal out of context. Then there are those, not elaborated, where this supremely confident person mentions, almost in passing, the times that she contemplated suicide. For people who have led conventionally regulated lives, *Dawns + Dusks* may read like romantic escape fiction, and for those who have never found a focus for their lives it may read like an organizational chart; but I cannot imagine that for any reader it will be less than contact by proxy—and very close, for a proxy—with a woman whose presence in a room enhances everyone else's sense of his own life.

I have written "woman" instead of "person" because Louise Nevelson is spectacularly a woman. Of course we are on dangerous ground here. Today there are armies of women ready to bristle, and armies of men ready to grow smug, when a woman who is an artist is described as a woman artist. The term has associations with the idea that women are short on certain major strengths and long on certain minor virtues when it could accurately be taken to imply a balance in a division where there are bound to be differences.

Louise Nevelson is an intuitional artist. It makes a great difference that she is also a disciplined one, but she is still first of all intuitional, as passage after passage describing her way of working proves. Intuition plays a great part in the art of many men also, but I think women are really better at it, and this book for me adds up to a vivid revelation of the romantic, intuitional creative spirit in action.

John Canaday

New York, May 26, 1976

DAWNS+DUSKS

*M*y theory is that when we come on this earth, many of us are ready-made. Some of us—most of us—have genes that are ready for certain performances. Nature gives you these gifts. There's no denying that Caruso came with a voice, there's no denying that Beethoven came with music in his soul. Picasso was drawing like an angel in the crib. You're born with it.

I claim for myself I was born this way. From earliest, earliest childhood I knew I was going to be an artist. I *felt* like an artist. You feel it—just like you feel you're a singer if you have a voice. So I have that blessing, and there was never a time that I questioned it or doubted it.

Some people are here on earth and never knew what they wanted. I call them unfinished business. I had a blueprint all my life from childhood and I knew exactly what I demanded of this world. Now, some people may not demand of life as much as I did. But I wanted one thing that I thought belonged to me. I wanted the whole show. For me, that is living.

I don't say life was easy. For forty years, I wanted to jump out of windows. But I did feel I had the strength and the creative ability. There was never any doubt about that. No one could move me till I got what I wanted—on my terms, on earth. And I do. And it did take, maybe not the greatest mind, but it did take courage. And it did take despair. And the hardship gave me total freedom.

People have said to me, "Aren't you glad you were born?" Well, I had no choice. I didn't ask to be born. Just think of the burdens we have at birth. We're born to people. We have labels. And we have to carry them all our lives without our choice. It's a hell of a thing to be born, and if you're born, you're at least entitled to yourself.

In my childhood there were great injustices. We were an immigrant family, foreigners in a Daughters of the Revolution town. And I think it must have made a great impression on me. I was four and a half when we came to Rockland, and that was such a WASP country. Now it's better. But think of 1905 when you have a name like BER-LI-AWSKY, and you come to Maine. Many of the people in Maine were very rich, believe it or not. And many of them had very beautiful homes. And they needed foreigners like I need ten holes in my head. So . . . it was difficult. I suppose the age that I was, maybe the sensitivities, it affected me in a certain way. I saw the injustices. I don't even say it was suffering, it was just that one was placed in a position from childhood that's unfair. Just totally unfair.

So I saw from the very beginning how one exploits another. And I recognized that the most important thing in my life was to claim myself totally. I was always independent. That I inherited. By the time I was nine, I had thoroughly decided I would never—in principle—work for anyone as long as I lived. I was gifted and I knew it, and I wasn't going to permit anyone on earth to take my true heritage. I felt I had the equipment to fulfill living life, and I don't think I wanted less. I wanted to fulfill life. And that's exactly what I'm doing. I claimed what I have. I still claim what I have. And you know, as long as we're aware, we have a right to that.

Everyone is entitled to recognize their full being. Male or female, the human being is entitled to that total heritage, no matter what. There's a corny expression that from an acorn a big oak tree grows. You can have that: that's your inheritance. Less than that . . . if you really believe in a power beyond, then you're cheating that power. They claim that we are created in the image and likeness of God. That takes my femininity away [laughing]. So anyway . . . if you do think like that, then you're cheating and selling cheap who you are created in the image and likeness of.

We underestimate what humans are, you see. When I hear people say "the common man" . . . *I hate that phrase.* You know, we hear it, writers have

used it, poets have used it. I think it's a great mistake. There's no such thing.
There's nobody that's common. I think that in every human being there is
greatness.

The tragedy on earth is that people are born into a certain environment.
Think of this. When you're born, you have two parents, usually. Now, those
parents are in a position to control every move we make, so already we've got
a ton of this on our heads. And then as we move on, we go to school; the
teacher has pets, and for some reason she may not like a student and can
destroy them. You see, the human relationships are deadly. Of course there's
the other side too—otherwise we couldn't live. But what I'm bringing out is
that from birth until you're grown, you have superiors. You're educated all
along the line, not necessarily by your parents, but by your schools, academic
training and all, in the strange way that you have to be humble to inherit the
earth. You're taught to be subservient to religion, subservient to the older
people, subservient . . . God knows . . . down the line.

You see, sometimes you have to turn about the things you are taught. You
have to stand on your two feet and claim your true heritage. What does that
mean? That means you belong to yourself. The fact that we can breathe is
really kind of a miracle, and so if you see that and work for that, you finally
find yourself claiming who you are, and you can only be a total human being
and be a human being to others when you know who you are . . . and you
have every right to that.

Now people might say, oh, aren't you selfish? Well, I don't know what
they mean. Who is more important in life than oneself? Your own life is all
lives. I feel that if we're self-centered—I don't mean in a bad sense—it's a
very healthy thing. Because if you're not self-aware you can't give. You have to
have within you to give. Now if you *want* to give somebody your life, that's
fine because that comes from you. As long as it is your choice and you
understand it, that's great. But if someone wants to take your life, you don't let
them have it. Or any part of it. If it's superimposed on you then you are not
recognizing your total being. The one thing you have to remember as long as
you live: your mother, your father, your sister, your brother, *nobody*, nobody
on earth is *your* center. *Your center* is *your center*. We humans can't
encompass everything. We can only encompass a radius around us. If a human
being permits anything to take them out of their center—which is the eye, the

third eye placed between the other two eyes, within—they are giving up their true human inheritance. And that is the only thing there is. The minute you give it up, you're not in command of yourself. You're not a total being.

That doesn't mean you have to be stubborn, that you don't have to do certain things in order to survive, to do certain things for other people. But it's *you* are the center. *You* are the moving person. When you have a center, you can help everybody. From that place you throw the ball of generosity. That is where I move from. Everything that I do, more or less, comes from that place.

When people lose their center, they go in for material things. But they can come back to it, sometimes with a difference, and sometimes they blossom more. I think we all fall, but some of us have something that we pick ourselves up and go on, to greater things. And I think the difference between not going on and going on is where life really fulfills itself. Life isn't one straight line. *Never.* Most of us have to be transplanted, like a tree, before we blossom.

$\mathcal{M}$y father came to America. And we came to America. I have one brother and two sisters. My brother's the oldest—my brother, then I. Anita's third. And Lillian's the baby. We were all born in Russia except Lillian.

My father's family had a lot of land. "Woods," I think they called it. And he had brothers and sisters, and almost all of them, especially the males, came to America. They had an uncle that was a so-called governor; he had the highest honors and position that our people could have in Russia at that time. It was rare. And he had no children, so he could adopt all these boys as his own so they didn't have to go into the army. So the other brothers must have started emigrating in the late 1880s, but my father stayed on to take care of his parents and the land. He was the last to go, in 1903.

My mother lived in the country in a small town near Kiev where my father's family owned land. And my father went to this village—he was a bachelor in his twenties, and his brothers had already come to America—and he was on a white horse. And he sees on the street this beautiful girl. She was only sixteen. And he sees her and he never wanted to marry, but he took one look and he found out who she was and where she lived and he fell desperately in love with her. Nothing on earth could stop him.

She liked another boy and she didn't want to get married because he pursued her so desperately, but he just was not going to take no for an answer. She had an older sister that lived in another small town and there was a river

Isaac Berliawsky family, Rockland, Maine (Louise on right)

between them, the Dnieper, and that river froze so they could go over the ice. And this was the one year in one hundred years that the river didn't freeze, so she couldn't get over on the other side.

So anyway, she married my father and then was unhappy with him. He was a handsome man, but he didn't suit her, and also I think it's hard to be happy when you're making a transition. A woman who should have been in a palace. I think that's my idea for myself . . . that she had to go to Rockland and struggle.

My father didn't go to New York because he had brothers that went through Canada. Don't forget this must have been a hundred years ago. So they came through Canada and they had enough money to stop in Waterville, Maine. One brother went to Baltimore but the other stayed in Canada. So the brother in Waterville told my father to come and visit him in America. But he wanted to run my father, and my father wasn't going to take that. The brother was ready to enslave him in labor, so my father got on the train and he gave what money he had left to the conductor and said, "Leave me off when the money runs out." So they left him off in Rockland, and he wasn't going to stay there. It was only to bring his family over.

I was about three when my father went to America, and my mother told me that for one half year I didn't speak. And they thought I had become deaf and dumb. We went to live with my mother's father and mother. And that was a small town outside of Kiev. I remember seeing my grandmother dyeing wool. Different colors with vegetable dyes. I have a faint recollection of the house, not much. I know that the stove wasn't like ours but was somehow built in the wall. Then I don't know how we left there, but I remember the trip to America. I remember a bit on the boat. There were barrels of these round water biscuits and evidently you could go and take them when you wished and I would go there and take some and pass them around.

Well, then we got to Liverpool, and I remember the depot. The lights, the big spaces, and people going and moving . . . and there on the shelves I saw every color of hard candies in jars. And then the lights—it was glass that had reflection. So it looked like heaven. Young as I was I remember this image, it made such an impression on me. It was very magical. It still is, because how many times are you moved to have an insight of that kind? An impact that even now, seventy years later, still thrills me.

In Liverpool we got the measles and were quarantined for six weeks. So we were already in living quarters, and we played with children on the street.

It was my first encounter with a doll that closed its eyes. I saw this child playing with it in the street. And when she'd lay it down, the eyes would shut. Well, we didn't see that in Russia. And I thought it was just magic. Actually I think that dolls are surrealistic. The translation . . . the translation of trying to make a doll a human almost gives it a mystical kind of thing. And to this day I think that dolls are unique.

But then Lillian was born and she was a baby, so I shied away from dolls. I guess I just didn't want to take care of anybody in that sense. I know if anyone wanted to get me a toy, I preferred a monkey. I had one and I remember it. It had a dark red body and the face was brown and I thought that was adorable.

I remember somehow being in Rockland. It must have been early spring. Because by fall we were speaking English. We spoke a little Russian when we came and Yiddish in the home and then learned English very quickly.

Now let me tell you about Rockland, Maine. It's on the east coast. Right on the water. And it's a small town. It was eight thousand when we got there. Eight thousand now. The ships and the boats would come there. It was kind of a little center. It still is a little center. If I was there now and I was seventy-six years old, I'd be an old lady. I'd be a fat lady. I wouldn't have my teeth. That's the way they are. First they don't get to be seventy-six. When I go home once in a while most of the people aren't there any more. But when I used to go home and see people even as far back as the 1940s, I didn't know who they were. And they were lovely-looking people when they were in school, but they got heavy and their teeth weren't taken care of, they were gray-haired and not dressed right. So you see, it's placement. Now here, in a city like this, the activity and excitement . . . I love New York.

Rockland was a WASP Yankee town, and look, an immigrant family pays a price. Even if you were Jesus Christ Superstar, you were still an outsider. My parents were outsiders in that sense. So I was an outsider. I *chose* to be an outsider and I knew what I had.

My father had to establish himself. He was a very loyal man to the family, and he did whatever he could, but until he established himself, he didn't know what he was going to do. I remember my mother saying that he was never lazy in Europe, yet when we first came, he lay in bed for months. He went through transition, not knowing what to do. And the language. All these things. Then

First house, on Linden Street, in the south end of Rockland, near the water. *Diana MacKown*

The house Isaac Berliawsky built next door. *Diana MacKown*

when he got started you couldn't stop him. Sooner or later he began feeling out—just like in Russia—about land. So he got land. And then he got lumber. And then he built houses. It wasn't in a minute. He felt it out.

The first place we lived was on C Street, near the Thorndike Hotel. Then my father bought, not too long afterwards, a house in the South End, near the water, that Mike eventually lived in. But it was old when he got it. Then he built the house next to it, so we moved into that one. We stayed there quite a long time, because I graduated, and Nevelson met me there.

In an article written not too long ago it said that I picked up things in my father's lumberyard. He had lumber and he had maybe a lumberyard, but it was a little out of Rockland itself and I never bothered. I just want to make it clear for the future so that students must not think because their father has a grocery store they're going to make groceries!

I always thought my father was a piece of genius. That has given me my strength. Now, that doesn't mean I adored him; I just knew how to judge him. And I'm not saying it lightly, because he was too hard for me, too busy. He was always so high-keyed. If you did this [knocking wood], he jumped. When he came home, it was like an engine. I always felt like it was a furnace downstairs going chuga-chuga-chug. So we didn't communicate much.

He adjusted, but my mother never did. I adored my mother. She was a brilliant woman, and she was a most beautiful woman. When we were growing up in Rockland, she dressed like for New York. She used to rouge her face and everything when they didn't do it. She brought that from the Old World. She had a great flair. But I knew she was very unhappy. I had great sympathy for her, because she was misplaced—on land, misplaced socially. She was misplaced in every conceivable way. She didn't want to get married either. Marriage made her very unhappy. So there was misplacement of love, misplacement of land, altogether. She just never adjusted. And she was sick all her life. She had a sense of humor, but she'd get into bed and stay for several weeks at a time. We used to have one doctor. Then we had two doctors, then three doctors. Then she went to Boston—that was the big city. Then she went to New York. And there was nothing we could do.

She was so ill-adjusted and was so beautiful that I never shed a tear when she passed away. I never felt that she was happy on earth. I never saw her happy. But I always felt so sympathetic to her that I was determined to open every front door—I like colonial ones, in the middle of the house. And to walk

Louise Berliawsky, age seven years

Crayon drawing, 6¾″ x 5½″, dated 1905, and signed. *Archives of American Art*

right through the door I didn't care if I had to build the house myself.

So I had two parents. Now that didn't make a happy home. I'm not glorifying it. Because when you get two attractive people—both high-keyed and both gifted and struggling with a new country . . . it wasn't an easy life. It was a goddamn struggle. But both parents had something. They were both very attractive people physically. And I believe that the physical is the geography of the being. My father loved antiques and things. And my mother knew fashion, she knew the line. And that gives me a feeling of rightness to do what I did. It wasn't a battle because it was right.

When we came here, my father and mother were very aware that it was a new world. Each one, it was told, had an equal opportunity. I don't think we think that now, but at that time, somehow this country was young and rich. Don't forget, in 1905, Teddy Roosevelt was president. Don't forget that this country was so rich in natural resources, and we've been exploiting it, the redwoods, the water, et cetera, and we've taken out the materials from the earth. But at that time, if one wanted to, there were great opportunities. At that time, don't forget, what you made, you had. There were no income taxes. And everything was fresh at that time.

So my parents believed the children, no matter what sex, should be educated. They had a son and three daughters and they felt we had the same opportunities that anyone had. And they began to give us every advantage. When I told them at an early age that I wanted to be an artist, he was as proud as he could be. And she was. And so they helped in every possible way. They helped me in every way. There was no problem. With them. So I must say that I didn't feel being a female was any handicap. I felt it was one's ability that counted. And I just thought I had it.

Who is an artist? I say, we take a title. No one gives it to us. We make our lives. You start when you're very young, say in school. And there you recognize that you have it. In the first grade, I already knew the pattern of my life. I didn't know the living of it, but I knew the line. I drew in childhood, and went on painting and moving and everything, daily. Daily and holidays too. I felt that that was my strength. And my good fortune was that many, many years ago, even in a small town in Maine, every teacher knew it too. As a child everybody knew that I had these two things. Pianissimo and fortissimo. Always. My teachers praised me. From the first day in school they said I'm an artist.

When I was about seven years old our art teacher came once a week and would demonstrate what she wanted us to do for the following week. This particular day she brought in her own crayoned drawing of a sunflower on paper and said that she wanted each of us to make a sunflower drawing for the next week as the assignment. I drew a large brown circle for the center and surrounded it by tiny yellow petals. When she reviewed the drawings she picked mine and held it up to the class and said it was the most original because I had changed the proportions of her drawing.

All the way through school I was fed by these art teachers. There were other problems, but that was not the problem. From the first day in school until the day I graduated, everyone gave me one hundred plus in art. Well, where do you go in life? You go to the place where you got one hundred plus.

You know, people always ask children, what are you going to be when you grow up? I remember going to the library, I couldn't have been more than nine. I went with another little girl to get a book. The librarian was a fairly cultivated woman, and she asked my little girl friend, "What are you going to be?" And she said that she was going to be a bookkeeper. There was a big plaster Joan of Arc in the center of the library, and I looked at it. Sometimes I would be frightened of things I said because they seemed so automatic. The librarian asked me what I was going to be, and of course I said, "I'm going to be an artist." "No," I added, "I want to be a sculptor, I don't want color to help me." I got so frightened, I ran home crying. How did I know that when I never thought of it before in my life?

As a young child I could go into a room and remember everything I saw. I'd take one glance and know everything in that room. That's a visual mind. You see, the eyes are marvelous. They're the finest of all our senses, the most intelligent. We have an insight. We call it the third eye, the eye between the two, and when we speak a million times a day we say, "I am going." We don't say, "My eyes are going," we say, "I (eye) am going" . . . I claim that the visual and the projection of the eye is the highest order that we humans are heir to. It's the quickest way of communicating and I think it's the most joyous.

. . . I think I could have been eleven or twelve. We lived in the South End, and we went to school practically in the North End. Which means a mile, anyway. Every morning we walked there, came home for lunch, went back, came home. But we'd have to run a little bit because of the time. I think we got out at twelve and had to be back at one. In spring, I remember, the trees were so rich, the foliage was so rich that when we were running through it, practically all we could see was this *green*, above our heads like umbrellas. *Big* umbrellas, weighing down. And you recognized that if a branch fell, it would *kill* you. There was a sense of insecurity about it. We accepted it, but I always felt a kind of terror. Of course we studied light and shade in Maine, in our art course, but it didn't really penetrate. It was only after I came to New York and studied art seriously that I could *reconstruct* nature. You recompose from nature into art and give it total form and you're never confused again.

We always had horses in Rockland. There weren't so many automobiles. And we had laboring horses, and some race horses. But there was one horse . . . I never did know who it belonged to, but we were coming home from school and going to school and I saw a black horse. It wasn't a race horse or a work horse. It might have been pregnant because it had a *big torso.* The horse was running wild, running alone without any harness or carriage. Maybe it got out of the stable for a moment. Because it was running and running, and this *marvelous* body . . . it seems to me that the torso was just bigger, not *taller,* but bigger than most of the horses I'd seen. And this *color* of black against nature of green . . . everything was in foliage, everything was in bloom . . . and this horse was *right* for this environment, because everything was oozing, and the speed of those legs and the hindquarters . . . they were *enormous* . . . and the stomach part was even bigger. And while the horse wasn't like a race horse with *long* legs, yet it had the *energy* of all of nature and had *symmetry* in its body. It had a *movement* no machine could match. I was alone, running to school, when I saw this. I was running the same way so I could watch the horse. I couldn't have been more than eleven or twelve, and I never forgot the image. I've never seen another horse that affected me that way.

Let's not forget this: evidently we can see a million horses, but *that* horse . . . we can have a million lovers, but *one* lover, and have a million dogs, but *one* dog. So it's always a selection. You don't select it and it doesn't select you. But it happens. It's a *marriage* of some sort. Because I remember as a child we had a little dog, a stray dog, and I fell in love with that little stray dog that came along. I was much younger then. And it was black. But the way that dog affected me . . . I have a dog, and I've seen *gorgeous* dogs, and I've seen what you call show dogs. I admire them, but they didn't *affect* me.

I think the same thing happens with people. I was a little older, let's say

Maine landscape, watercolor, 4¼″ x 6¾″, by Louise Berliawsky, dated 1916

Maine landscape, watercolor, 4¼″ x 6¾″, by Louise Berliawsky, dated 1916

about sixteen. There was a neighbor who had a relative that came from Camden. And this boy was known to be a good-for-nothing. He didn't work and he used to come to visit. He was slender and already looked decadent. Blue eyes. And I remember looking in his eyes and seeing depths which I've never seen again.

I don't remember names, I don't remember dates. I've always had a block about names, and I think it was the whole background. My parents believed in education, and so we took piano lessons. Now I was very self-conscious and very aware of the difference in environments. And the music teacher was the highest society in Rockland. They lived on Middle Street, the best street in Rockland, in a big house. So she was about six foot two, and she looked like Mrs. Roosevelt, and her home was one of the showplaces there, and the family of Bird in Maine was very elegant. I must have been eleven and was at her home to take a lesson and as I walked in, before I could sit down, she introduced me to a man, very attractive, from New York. Well, I had never met anyone from New York before, and I remember turning red and from there on I never listened to names.

I was already in high school. One day the principal of the school came into art class with a guest. What was considered the finest things and the finest taste in Maine at that time was the colonial house. So I was working in watercolor on this colonial interior when the principal and guest came in to observe the class. Behind my back while I was working the guest just started to roar. Over the mantel, in the middle of my interior, I had painted a portrait of an ancestor that looked like a true ancestor of myself, and not a colonial one. Eventually I learned from my art teacher that the guest had laughed because I had not accepted the myth of George Washington, hook, line, and sinker.

Needless to say that didn't please me. But it gave me food for thought. You see, you don't choose. From the day you are born there is a pattern, not of your own conscious choosing. I would like to go so far as to say, like an architect of this kind of thinking, that in the future you will claim your true heritage and you will have a choice of taking a name. You will have a choice . . . not having yourself stamped. You will choose. When we're free of this kind of thinking, we'll be free of the other things that surround it.

In retrospect, I think the one thing that kept me going was that I

Watercolor, 8½″ x 11″, dated 1918, and signed. *Archives of American Art*

Living room of Linden Street house, watercolor, 6″ x 9¼″, by Louise Berliawsky, dated 1918.
Archives of American Art

Library of Linden Street house, watercolor, 6″ x 8¾″, by Louise Berliawsky, dated 1918. *Archives of American Art*

Bedroom of Linden Street house, watercolor, 6″ x 9″, by Louise Berliawsky, dated 1918.
Archives of American Art

Kitchen of Linden Street house, watercolor, 6″ x 9″, by Louise Berliawsky, dated 1914. *Archives of American Art*

wouldn't be appeased. You know, maybe you see in little children that they're quiet. You give them candy and they're happy. But some of us, even when we were little children, wanted something else—what life really gives. Something that would justify our being here. And I meant it. And I would take nothing less. I wasn't satisfied to be on earth—and I don't say accept the good things or the bad things—I wasn't satisfied with any of the things. I wanted one thing. And not only that, my brain only went to one thing. Art was all that mattered to me, at all times right from the very beginning. I don't like to read fairy tales and never did. I didn't like to write poetry when most girls did. I wasn't the greatest academic student. I studied geometry, and that didn't make me know myself better. I learnt the world, so to speak, totally through art.

When I was entering high school, you didn't have to take drawing. You selected it if you wanted it. So of course I selected art and I loved it. Loved my drawing teachers. I never had a moment when I questioned it. It always seemed so right. For instance, I've always been a little cold. I was born in a cold country and I was raised in a cold country. And I always thought the art room was warmer than all the rooms in the school. I was more comfortable in it. I'm sure it didn't have more heat, but it always seemed to be warmer. And so I couldn't wait to get to that room, and I was very active there. I would stay after class. It wasn't until years later that it dawned on me that *I generated my own heat in that room.*

Now I might be cold on a winter day, and I'll go into my studio and I get warmed up and I say, well, what is this? This is no warmer. But just being there warms me. So I decided that there's a kind of energy a person himself creates. We generate heat towards the thing we like or the thing we are close to. You see, I knew all my life that that's where I wanted to be.

I liked the art teachers, too. I think they all went to Pratt at the time. And they all seemed different from the rest of the teachers, more human. They looked different and behaved differently. And they had a distinction about their clothes.

So I loved this particular teacher. Her name was Miss Cleveland, and she came from Camden. I think she also went to Pratt. A woman about fifty-five. Never married. Conventionally she certainly wasn't beautiful, she was an old maid and behaved like it, yet she had something that no one around me had. She was gracious. And what appealed to me even then was, she had a beautiful purple hat and purple coat. For Rockland, that was something. And so I said, "Miss Cleveland, you have a beautiful hat and coat." So we started to talk about it—she loved to talk—and she said, "Well, I bought the hat because I *liked* it. And then I found a coat." Instead of the reverse. Well, that struck me. It was so wonderful to have that little hat on your head that size, and then to search, because she was rather a large woman, for a coat to match the hat. So that pleased me. I think she was right. It's like if you have a tiny jewel, say a pin. And then you get a dress for it and do your hair for it. And you make a whole great picture because you want to enhance that one thing.

When I was about fourteen, I bought a hat frame and some linen and somehow got it on the frame. It was like pleats. Then I made stenciled butterflies and painted them. Well, I don't know how I did it. I was the only one in Rockland that ever thought of doing it. I wore it. All the time. It was a brimmed hat, but I mean, in retrospect, what made me do it? I think it's the funniest thing I did. I wore it to school every day, and no one said a word about it.

When I was in the ninth grade, I was blooming. I was as tall as I am and exciting. And I was captain of the high school basketball team. And darling, all I had to do was take the ball and throw it in the basket—I never missed. I was vice-president of the glee club and I sang, and we went out of Rockland to the environments around us and no matter what was taking place, I was always a part of it. Now really, I didn't seek that. There was something about my presence that demanded it. And I was a yes woman—a yes girl and always said yes.

My mother said to me, "You know, Louise, you permit people to use you." And I said, "Yes, mother, if I didn't feel that I could be used I think that would be the end of me." I suppose I qualified for these things because all these things I was equipped for. But I wasn't pushing in that direction. I was extremely shy in some ways.

I recall that I didn't get too involved emotionally with local color. I knew I was very emotional, but I guess my emotions were in another place. I was interested in art. I was interested in music. And I liked people and I even liked to gossip about people . . . and yet I was aware of a depth somewhere that I didn't feel in others. Somehow I was removed as I was growing up. So I guess my mother had never seen me get too involved over people's feelings.

Well, I used to go on errands to Littlefields, that was a wholesale place, to

Rockland High School basketball team (Louise Berliawsky, center), 1916

get fresh eggs and so on. And one day we heard that the man who waited on
me in the store . . . his wife had died and left him with four children. And
they said that every day since she had died, he was found at her grave. Where
he lived was a very isolated place. It wasn't in the little city of Rockland; it
was further out, way out in the country.

Well, a short while later we heard that he told his housekeeper not to
come, and he locked the doors. And he gave each child a different time to pass
away. And he sat there and wrote down—this child took so long, and how it
passed away. And he went through the whole process with all four children.
He said that he could not conceive of leaving these children on earth, and
since he wasn't going on, he felt it was better to take them with him.

Now, we also learned what I hadn't known before, that this man came
from a distinguished English family, and the woman, his wife, evidently had
been a maid in the house. And he desperately adored her. So when they
married they left England and came to America. They were probably given a
little pension. And, you see, they took a place that was isolated. These two
people were like one, evidently. She got ill and died. But he couldn't live
without her.

Since I'm not a writer, I'm not able to say it more clearly, which I would
like to. But one day I was running home from school for lunch (you know, it's
always running) . . . I was running south, and here came five hearses. One big
one for the father. Then the oldest child, next. The other three, next. The
black hearses, and this quiet procession moving . . . I've never *seen* anything
like it. Black horses, of course, and the quietness and all. And remembering
what I had already heard, and probably read in the *Courier-Gazette*. I must
have been a sophomore. Fourteen. When I got in the house, I just shed a ton
of tears. And my mother couldn't believe it. She was overwhelmed to see my
power of feeling. Well, at my age now, seventy-six, I still think it is probably
the truest form of tragedy.

Now think of a small town. You know, the main street, the buildings—
two stories if we were lucky. All the same, brick or stone. Then think of five
carriages. Think of the rhythm of five carriages over the cobblestones. And
think of my own age of receptivity. It hadn't been *jaded* with anything yet.
And so the impact for me was *pure unadulterated tragedy*. I *still* think so.

Then, location plays such a part. Certain environments give one a feeling
of innocence, and I think I am probably justified in saying that *that* was a

virginal place. And it was a moment in time that . . . nothing on that level ever happened to me again. It really had nothing to do with me, and it affected my life more, in a way, than things that *did* have to do with me. Which makes me think . . . when we are moved, it can be something that happens to us, or it can be just an observation. And an observation can be more meaningful to your life than something that is really a part of it. Let me put it this way. As much as we know about psychiatry and life and all, there are nuances that *scream louder* than the thing that's obvious.

A man who was *that* thoughtful . . . I am still overwhelmed by that kind of great rationality. And by seeing the whole thing. As I sit here now and think of it, that was a moment of true vision. I am sure that nobody else was so affected by it. I saw it as a tragic act, a tragic totality in pure essence.

*B*y the time of graduating from high school, I weighed about what I do now, and I had big arms and big legs. They weren't out of proportion, but they were biggish. (I'm five feet seven and a half inches.) And I related myself to the wonderful neoclassic colonial houses in Maine, like the captains' houses that had four big columns that were white. I felt that I was related, that my arms and legs related to those columns. So I couldn't take a lesser house. For instance, a lot of houses through New England had fences and flowers, and they were white, but I didn't feel in tune with cozy things, I felt related more to the big classic-stately. Those big pillars and the purity of the houses and the squareness and the cleanness, and the windows (they're not many) are put in the right places like eyes. And they've got a front entrance, a door that opens right to the front. I still think they're magnificent, and I'd stack it against anything.

I met Nevelson, who was a New York sophisticated man, when I was between seventeen and eighteen. Usually you say seventeen until you are eighteen, but let's say I was between seventeen and eighteen because it was the graduation year. This was during the First World War. The Nevelson family in the Wall Street section were in the shipping business. And the government took their ships for the war. Well, some of them were damaged. And we had shipyards in Maine. So they brought some of their ships to Maine. And that is how I met him.

There were four brothers, and they were all in this business. Charles

Louise Berliawsky, 1919, Rockland, Maine

Nevelson was the youngest and Bernard was the oldest, sixteen years older than he. There was that span. There were two brothers in between. All of the brothers were born in Russia. They came from Riga, that's almost nearer I think to Germany. Their father, like my father, had land. Nevelson became a citizen only during the war. Being in the shipping business, they were doing big business through their associations and they had entrance to the president, who at the time was Woodrow Wilson.

They had two offices down on Broadway, and I'll give you the numbers. One was 42 Broadway. That's way down in the Battery. The building is still there. That was the Nevelson Brothers Shipping. Then they formed another company, 120 Broadway—that company was called the Polish American Navigation Company. It was a national company for Poland. The president was Paderewski's wife's son. He and some other names of distinction from their country got together to have a fleet of ships. And they knew that the Nevelson brothers were rising very fast in the shipping business, so they came to them and formed this company.

I think it's a fantasy that one half century later Howard Lipman invited me downtown to lunch. He and his partners have a floor-through in a building and, being art collectors, the rooms were full of art. I walked in and there's my work big as life. And the address—120 Broadway!

What happened was, Bernard Nevelson, the older one, came to Maine, and he came with his captain, a Frenchman, for the ship. And they stayed at the Thorndike Hotel. He was interested enough to want to know if there were some people of our kind in this city, and he met my father, and so I suppose there were some kind of inquiries made. I don't quite remember. And I got an invitation to come to the hotel for dinner.

So I was very nervous, because I had never been in a hotel and I had never had dinner in a hotel. But you know, my curiosity got the better of me, and I did go. I was frightened because the captain was a Frenchman with a big beard, and I had not met anything like him; also there was a ship . . . I should have known that that was legitimate, but I guess I wasn't prepared for it. I was afraid that the ship would go off and I'd be on it and all sorts of fantasies.

So then Mr. Bernard Nevelson went back to New York. But I must say in all depth that he must have seen something about me, because after he met me he never let me go. He wrote letters to me. Of course he had already told me he had a wife and they were about to have their first baby. She was in the early forties and he was probably in the late forties, and they didn't want children for about ten years. She was a nurse and they saw themselves as intellectuals—intelligentsia. He probably even more than she. So when he wrote me a few letters I didn't answer them, because I had *read* about these things, and I had heard about robber barons having young mistresses and so forth, and I wasn't about to venture into that kind of life. But then I got a letter saying that his brother Charles was coming this trip instead of him, to see about their ship. And then the brother did come to town and telephoned me and asked me to go out for dinner. And I knew that I was in the driver's seat because of the letters.

I took my mother into the kitchen and I said, "Mr. Nevelson is here, and he's going to propose to me this evening and I'm accepting." After I had educated her that I was not going to be married and live a conventional life, because I was going to be an artist. It was a very important time in my life, because I had just graduated from high school and was ready that fall to go to Pratt Art Institute. Well, my mother was bewitched and bewildered. Once I say no and once I say yes and wasn't it hard for her to go along with me? But she trusted me. She said, "You know, it's going to be a hard life, being an artist, to live that way." I said, "It isn't how you live, it's how you finish." And that's exactly what I'm doing.

Nevelson was a New York man, older than I. I knew very little. He was gentle in a way with me, as best he could be, which means he was probably upper middle class. And I explained very carefully that I wanted to study art, that I was going to pursue a creative life, and he said that was all right and there was no reason I couldn't continue. We could still get married.

I suppose I was a little afraid of New York City and I thought—companionship. I don't think it was cut and dried. I think a lot of things entered. The point was that we had decided not to have children and that I was just to continue my studies.

This is what's amazing—when I wanted to study with Estelle Liebling and it was fifty dollars a lesson, he didn't complain. But I soon recognized that within their circle you could know Beethoven, but God forbid if you were Beethoven. You were not allowed to be a creator, you were just supposed to be an audience. They thought they were terribly refined. They were in the shipping business, but all their friends were sort of Russian intelligentsia . . . musicians, doctors. I think probably at that time that was a step ahead of just business, and they couldn't stand just business types. They couldn't stand, for instance, if people—no matter how rich—were, according to their standards, *crude*. If you were refined, you had to have one little flower on a plate. You couldn't have a plate full of flowers. You had to have a little diamond, never a big one. Nineteenth-century Victorian concepts. Now the Nevelsons were very friendly with their neighbors in New York. These two brothers had a store down in Maiden Lane which was famous for their diamonds, so he, Charles, picked out a ring, an engagement ring. It was one carat. Well, you know, a one-carat ring for a rich man didn't seem very impressive (and also I don't think I even liked the setting), but they thought it would be vulgar to do otherwise. You see, people think that a big diamond is vulgar. I don't, I think a great big diamond can be beautiful. I don't particularly want a big diamond. See the difference? But I don't say it's vulgar because that's a convention, too. Well, everything they did was on that level, other than buying a big house and having a Pierce Arrow.

I saw through that. That's all so superficial. And I think having been brought up in the country, also, knowing pretty much what I was about to do, I couldn't quite reconcile myself to think that that was the height of life. I was a creator. I knew that art was what I wanted. I wasn't impressed with what I call middle-class culture. So right from the beginning I was determined *not* to stay in this environment. Now if you've lived in the country and you think like I do, you think deeper probably than here in the city.

It took two years before I married Nevelson. I was engaged for a year. At that time, anyway, you didn't get married that fast. In 1918 he invited us—my mother and me—to come to New York as his guests. We came by train to New York and stayed at the Martha Washington. Nevelson took us around and we went to the St. Regis and the Century Club and roof gardens all over. That was about three weeks. It was the first time I had come to the city. Then I came again a little later, went home. Then I got married June the twelfth at the Copley-Plaza in Boston. Nevelson and his brothers came from New York, and I with my mother and father and family came from Maine.

We were married. Then we went off to New Orleans. Then we came back to New York and took a second honeymoon in Cuba, because they also had ships there. And then we settled in New York.

Somehow I knew I was coming to New York from the beginning. I've lived here all my adult life, summer and winter, for over fifty years. And you

Louise Nevelson, 1922,
New York City

know, they talk about the dirt in New York. Well, for me it's so opulent, rich. It's the richest city in the world. I love the architecture, all these big mountainous buildings. If I take you up on the roof of 29 Spring Street you'll see Wall Street, the World Trade Center—grandeur, grandeur. I think New York is so vital.

Now the city and I have a lot in common. But when I first got here I thought it didn't move fast enough—it was a slower city. There were high buildings, though. The Singer Building down in Wall Street. The Woolworth Building. The Flatiron Building. I cared for the Flatiron Building. But more than that I remember there were private houses, *big* private houses from 34th Street to 57th Street. The Vanderbilts, the Huntingtons. Then that big Tiffany building on Madison, and that seems to have stamped itself most strongly on my mind at that time. That was the true New York for that period.

I was active in New York. I studied all the time. I was very shy at that age, and I knew I had to free myself. So I began to study voice professionally with Estelle Liebling, who was the coach for the Met and a very celebrated singer. I wanted to study dramatics too, not to be an actress but for these other reasons. And so there was an ad in the paper. Princess Matchabelli had started a dramatic school with Frederick Kiesler. She was a great beauty. She had been married to the great poet von Hofmannsthal, but then she fell in love with this Georgian prince and left him, and when I met her here in America, she was married to the Georgian prince, who was Matchabelli and who didn't have five cents. He was a little bowlegged and shorter than she, and eight years younger. But he had great nobility in his being. And in spite of not having money, he raised money for all the refugees from his country. He became later a great authority on perfume.

Princess Matchabelli had been the star of the Max Reinhardt theater in Berlin. She was brought here because she was in *The Miracle* for Reinhardt. Kiesler had been associated with Reinhardt's conception of new stage setting—he was twenty-six, I think, when he first did theater in the round. So he and Princess Matchabelli knew each other from Berlin, and they were very good friends. They had formed this theater group in Brooklyn, in a brownstone. And I called up and made an appointment for myself. I don't think there were more than about six or eight students.

So I studied music with the best teachers, and dramatics with the best teachers. I heard Rachmaninoff play, and I went to hear Krishnamurti. I went to hear Kreisler. I saw Martha Graham dance in the beginning. You see, I had a long-range view of my life. It pleases me that what I studied, not as a scholar but out of sheer necessity, has really played quite a part in my life. I was branching out and reaching out in many directions, but always with a difference, because my root was art and creation. And if I was going to say what I knew I wanted to say, I had to know from any avenue, from any direction, just how to say it. It was almost like a circle with many numbers. I had the foresight to understand that all of these arts were pretty much one. All of them were essential; one supported the other. I felt I was fortifying the whole structure.

I've been a searcher, I'll tell you. I did search and do search. I'm not a student. I've never thought of myself as an intellect, but I have had strong desires. My desire was really to delve into life. We can tap it and say reincarnation, we can say metaphysics, we can say a lot of things. But that is not the ultimate. And so that's why they sing, oh, sweet mystery, you know. It's still unknown. I feel even at this point that if I could find an added dimension I would pursue it.

I remember that it was in the paper that Krishnamurti was going to give a lecture in Town Hall. I already leaned toward metaphysics and had read that he rejected the superimposition of being labeled a Messiah. He was moving from his whole center. And he wanted to free humanity so that each individual could claim their total being. And he is still communicating on that level.

I went alone and I got an aisle seat, say eight rows back in the middle. So I was sitting there and when I saw him on the platform, he was not too tall, he was standing, very slender, wore a white outfit. Black hair and of course *piercing* black eyes. And when he spoke—I have never had this experience, I saw his voice coming, not through his lips, but through the heart. I saw a vision of moving lips superimposed on his heart, which was a visual projection outside of him but placed in front of his heart. That was the strangest experience I ever had. And it lasted during the whole lecture. Years later he was at the Washington Irving High School on 16th Street and I went. After all these years, he was still giving people their true heritage, if they wanted to take it.

I knew I had to claim my true heritage, or I couldn't go on. The only thing was that I was now a mother. Soon after Mike was born in 1922 I went into a depression, right down to the tip of my toe. Here I had a son, and I didn't feel like living. I just felt like I was lost.

One day I walked down 57th Street, and at the time they had many stores with antique furniture. Well, somewhere along the line I spotted, like a sunburst, two antique French chairs in the window. They had yellow satin covers with no design at all. The shade of yellow and the touch of satin and the softness of that satin was an instantaneous healing. It cured me more than anything else could have cured me.

I do believe that sound and color are great healers. Did I ever tell you about my experience with the Noh robes, Diana? It must have been later, the late 1920s, say a year or two before I went to Europe to study. And things weren't so good. Already the Depression was beginning to take hold slowly on the country. Now the Nevelson Brothers Company, Diana, don't forget that their ships had been used for cargo during World War I, and when the war was over they had decided to take their ships and convert them for a new activity. They bought banana plantations in Nicaragua, began putting in railroads, and were shipping the bananas through Galveston, Texas, for America. Along came the United Fruit Company, which was a powerful monopoly, and made them an offer. They said, "We want to buy you out. If you don't sell to us, we'll break you." They rejected the offer and the United Fruit Company put them out of business.

So we were coasting. And I couldn't take the activity of moving and moving, disrupted daily and not in an interesting way. And I want to tell you something, I just didn't think life was worth living. You know how we humans get into suspended animation? Like a trance—this has happened to me a few times. You're so unhappy that you get frozen and you don't even know you're unhappy. And I saw no way of breaking this state of mind.

I didn't live very far from the Metropolitan Museum. There was a new building—108 East 91st Street—and before it was finished I, we, took an apartment in it. It wasn't my dream. But it was near the Met, so I walked to the museum one day and walked in and they had an exhibition of Japanese Noh robes. Let me say that there are things in us that we find parallel outside us, so these Noh kimonos . . . each robe was a universe in itself. I can tell you exactly where they were. The exhibition was on the south side on the balcony, and the manikins didn't have any heads, and I went upstairs and I looked at them—the forms—and then I looked at the material. Some had gold cloth with medallions, and the cloth was so finely woven that the likes of it I never saw, and then the medallion was gold so it was gold on gold. I looked and I sat

down without thinking and I had a barrel of tears on the right eye and a barrel
of tears on the left eye . . . and then my nose was running so there was
another barrel of that, and I wanted to go to the bathroom, so there was
another barrel. Everything was open. And then I knew and I said, oh, my God,
life is worth living if a civilization can give us this great weave of gold and
pattern. And so I sat there and sat and wept and wept and sat.

The thing that hit me was that they used it with such elegance. It was the
reverse of what people think, that gold material was a little vulgar. It was
made out of the thinnest of sheer-thin thread, it was so fine. So that the light
and shade were of that refinement. It was the height of human refinement, and
beyond that it would fall apart. And I thought, well, if there's been a
civilization of this development, then we have to recognize that there is a
place on earth that is an essence. I went home and it gave me a whole new life.

I had recognized right from the beginning that truly I didn't have very
much in common with my husband. I was never married in the true soul sense.
Oh, he was very sweet with the child. But under the turmoil of my life at that
given time, I was kept in a highly nervous state and if ever I had an inferiority
complex—that was the time.

In their group, it was fashionable to give your wife who had had a baby a
diamond bracelet. And so when Mike was born I got this diamond bracelet.
Well, of course it didn't appeal to my kind of thinking, but I accepted it
anyway. Now I went to visit a friend, and my mother was in town, and we
both took the car, the Peerless, to the Bronx. And when we sat down to play
cards, I noticed I didn't have my diamond bracelet. So I ran down to look, and
sure enough, it was lying right on the dashboard in full sight, and people were
walking right by. I couldn't believe it, so I grabbed it and put it on and went
upstairs. And felt what a blessing that was. I didn't care so much about the
diamond bracelet as I did about the finding of it.

There were so many things. Too many frustrations and disturbances all
together. But I caught on after a while, and then when I saw everything I was
determined to put an end to this sort of imprisonment.

I saw in the paper that this girl was on trial, because she wanted to go to a
party and her husband aggravated her, and he was sitting on the windowsill
and she threw him out. Gave him a little push. And I thought, there but for the
grace of God go I. And then I thought, I can't stay here because I'll do

something desperate. I must get out of this. So I began working toward that end. The only thing that I think saved my life was work because there was always a straight line there. I found that this was my stability.

When Mike was four I went to Boothbay Harbor one summer where they had an art school. And the director that was running it came up to me and said—he felt that I wasn't ready for his school—"I'd be glad to give you back your tuition. You don't have to stay." So I said, "No, I'll stay," and he said, "All right." So a few weeks later he selected my painting and said that it was the most vital because it was so dynamic and colorful. Now had I left when he suggested, I would have felt so defeated. But I stayed. I never ran.

I studied with the Baroness Rebay in the late twenties, when I was living at 108 East 91st Street. I knew her when she was only here a very short time. She already had her studio at Carnegie Hall, and right away she invited me to study with her. She gave me private lessons as long as I wanted them. She kept me on the skull for a long time, but she would be working with collage elements herself. And soon after she had a big show of these things at Wildenstein's on Fifth Avenue. And then in no time she got a commission to do a portrait of Solomon Guggenheim, so she got very busy with him. She began not too much later to build that museum. The Museum of Non-Objective Art, which later became the Guggenheim.

Now the Museum of Modern Art was just being formed, on 57th and Fifth, 730 Fifth Avenue, the Heckscher Building. They didn't yet have a building of their own. And I went up there frequently to see their exhibitions. We were beginning to get that art from Europe. Picasso had appeared, and Matisse, and that whole movement was *breaking*. I saw the first Picassos and it gave me a definition of structure of the world and every object in the world.

Without Picasso giving us the cube, I would not have freed myself for my own work. But suppose I *had* made these without Picasso, say one hundred years ago? No one would look at them. They wouldn't have any meaning. So Picasso changed our thinking and he gave us structure. Of course when you recognize that, you can vary it. But that is your foundation.

Duchamp, in his *Nude Descending a Staircase*, used Cubism and Futurism. Perfect. Now, Duchamp was a young man when the Armory Show was on in America in 1913. And that picture baffled America and baffled the world. It was for us a very new image. But when I saw it at the Museum of Modern Art, many years ago, I read it. Now, I never study paintings. I see them or I don't. And I saw the nude descending the staircase, simple as that.

Meaning, of course, that I recognized variations of the cube in different positions on the canvas, the recognizable parts of the nude translated into Cubism. The combination of movement with the cube baffled us, because we had not seen it before.

Many years later I dreamt about that painting, not wanting to or even consciously thinking about it, and in my dream the nude was *really* walking down the stairs. The same nude, not a figure of reality but these cubes in actual movement—physical movement. And in my dream I had more color than in the original. In the original it was in ochres surrounded by dark broken lines. I dreamt of it in opaque colors, dark Indian reds, dark greens, almost blackish colors, and that is the way I remembered it. I held that image for many years until I saw it again when it was permanently installed in the Philadelphia Museum and found it was in variations on ochres. And I was surprised. I had lived with the thought that the dream image was the reality until I saw it again. I think it's important that I tell you this because I don't think that enough is known about the creative mind. And I'm wondering why this creative mind in its dream superimposed something on the original. That's an important question.

I went up to the museums often in the early thirties. That was how I met Eilshemius. There was a man at the museum, a little old man, Mr. Trent, and he said, "You know, a friend of mine, Mr. Eilshemius, is a very lonely man and he's a very fine artist, and I would love it if you would be kind enough to pay him a visit, because he does very beautiful work." And he gave me the address, East 57th. And I said, "All right, thank you." And at that time I walked over, rang the bell, and went in and visited Eilshemius. And I found him a delightful man.

He spoke on poetry, on music, on composition. And he was an innocent—though he had traveled all over the world. And I don't think he was quite of this world as we understand it. A lot of people claimed he was eccentric. I felt he was very civilized and very wonderful, and I thought he was an attractive man, cultured—and then he had marvelous hands, and a wonderful face, and you know, he was very aristocratic-looking. The whole environment was magnificent. You could see the remnants of a great and beautiful home. The Eilshemiuses were a distinguished Dutch family. When the Vanderbilts rode with four horses, they rode with eight. Well, the house was full of his work, and the paintings were disintegrating. I saw and I was overwhelmed with these paintings. And of course I bought a piece right away, a little one. I bought one whenever I could. I thought the color and the vitality was great.

Another time I went into Dudensing, on 57th Street, that was *the* gallery of the time, and he was giving Eilshemius a show. I went into the show and there was Eilshemius looking at his paintings. There was one painting of ladies sitting on a bench. His people defied gravity. Wasn't that marvelous that they didn't need *terra firma* [knocking wood]? And he went up and he said, "Now you move over. I told you not to get off that bench. You sit where I put you." He had a whole conversation with these people on the bench. You see, Eilshemius was absolutely caught in his pictures. When he painted a picture, that was the reality more than this world.

He was a lonely man—and later he was hit by a car. And eventually they put him in Bellevue. But to my way of thinking, he had every reason for his kind of thinking. I never found him eccentric. He was an essence himself.

So I had studied art for many years; I was already aware that we had Cubism. The teachers that I had at the League were not of the modern movement. And I knew that in France and so forth there were these great movements, and I was very interested to be of the present time instead of the past. So I was ready. I had heard that the greatest teacher in the world at the time was Hans Hofmann, in Munich. So I had a talk with my mother, and she wasn't feeling well. I said to her, "Look, I can't leave now because you may pass away, the way things are." And as ill as she was, she said, "Louise, you must go. You always wanted to continue in your art. If I don't survive, it will make no difference. You go and study. We'll send you an allowance, and we'll take care of Mike and see that he has everything he needs." She said, "Look, you don't have to stay married. Before that you were so vital." By Christ, she sensed it. I was crippled up, and I knew what it was. If you have got a living force and you're not using it, nature kicks you back. The blood boils just like you put it in a pot. My mother was very sympathetic—she thought I had lost my soul. She saw the difference, and she had suffered through her own life. And so she was the one who really gave me the courage to take my freedom.

Here's the way I feel. No more marriages for me. Because I recognized the bondage. I think romance is great, and I think love affairs are marvelous, and I certainly think sex is here to stay, and I love it. As long as you meet as companions and you perform as lovers, that's fine. But the minute you get that

LN, 1931, New York City,
just before trip to Germany

two-dollar paper, a marriage license, that becomes a business—it's a partnership. And not only that, it gives the mates the privilege of all barriers down, and for God's sakes who can handle that! It's a lot of work and it's not that interesting. I wouldn't marry God if he asked me.

You see, I hate the word *compromise*. As I understand the word, the minute you compromise something's down. I knew that I needed to claim my total life. That means my total time for myself. I had to have totality. Night and day. Because very often at night, when I went to sleep, my figures would move as if they were real people. This was later, in the late thirties, and I was working in big pieces, of plaster. They were not realistic as we understand figures; still they had some part of the figure concept. And at night while dreaming I could see them as if electricity was in them, lighting them up, and I could see all of them moving in a world, in their world of reality. It gave me the feeling that there was a subterranean world, even if it was a dreamworld, where those bodies had a life of their own. So it was a dimension. It freed me that I wasn't just thinking of a work of art, a piece of work. That they had a life of their own. Well, now under those circumstances, let us say, had I not lived alone at that time, there would have been other intrusions. Maybe delightful, but they would have been intrusions nevertheless.

I do claim almost all of my life. I have always done that to a great degree, particularly my adult life. I think anyone that claims less for themselves is very sad, because that's the first thing that we have a right to—to claim ourselves while living ourselves. But I think that artists of any dimension have blind spots. They have to. Nature pads you and blinds you. I don't think I realized the price that would be demanded for what I wanted. I've been so lonely for long periods of my life that if a rat walked in I would have welcomed it. I remember one day I was sitting in the park, on Union Square. It was on a Saturday, and a group of men had a pint of whiskey and were passing it around. Then they'd talk about their wives and children, whether they had a fight or whether they didn't, et cetera. And I realized then that I was so lonely in my soul, that this was a society, they got together, took a drink, it was like a club. Not a fancy club, it was their club. And I realized that deep down in my soul, how lonely and alone I felt. But I never doubted that my life would fulfill itself. I must say that, or I wouldn't have had the courage.

I believed in my work and the joy of it. You have to be with the work and the work has to be with you. It absorbs you totally and you absorb it totally.

Everything must fall by the wayside by comparison. You see, humans have it in themselves really to be monistic. We have one God really . . . they never deny there was one head, that we are one being, and we have one love affair, and the others are secondary. And if you're an artist, truly that is paramount. That must be paramount.

Nothing—friendship, love, or anything—will come to such a harmony or unity as you come to in your work. Every day people think of having a love affair . . . I can tell you that I think it is exciting, but it's not the everlasting quality that art is, that creation is.

Then you see a friend, you say hello and good-bye. I like to speak to you as friends. And then, for no reason, I'll say, "Go to hell." And you say, "Why did you say that?" And there's an explosion. But that doesn't happen here. You see, here it is always harmony if you know how to give it harmony. Now I have a son who is a sculptor and I have three grandchildren and a great-grand-daughter. And they are wonderful. But the work that you do every day is something else, right here, and in you; it's something else. The work and you are one, the work is a living example, it's just as living as you are. It's your reflection.

I am closer to the work than to anything on earth. That's the marriage.

*W*hen I went to Europe for the first time, in 1931, I was desperate. I was going through a tough time emotionally, and it broke. Everything broke, and so here I was. It wasn't only art, it was so many psychological problems, motherhood and separation and the struggles within myself. I was caught at that moment in a broken marriage. Everything had collapsed and it was of my own choosing in a way, but that didn't make it easier. On the contrary, it made it harder. I felt myself without rudders, and I felt that I had no *terra firma.* So I was fighting desperately for a reality. And I went to anything I could think of, including vegetarianism, including all the isms that were available, to try to get a moment of peace. Not as a student—I didn't want to study anything— but out of despair. I had to find something to give me an anchor.

So when I went to Europe that first time, I really began to understand the cube. I had begun to recognize it in the late 1920s, but when I went to Hofmann in 1931 in Germany, I recognized it, I identified it, and it gave me the key to my stability. I had already delved into metaphysics (Krishnamurti) and I found that they had their symbols. Now, according to metaphysics, thinking is circular. The circle is the mechanics of the mind. It is a mind that turns and turns. It doesn't solve anything really. But when you square the circle, you are in the place of wisdom. There you are enlightened. And that's instantaneous. So Cubism already paralleled what I had selected in metaphysics and it gave me law. Not law, legal. I'm talking about order in a visual sense. It gave me definition for the rest of my life about the world. Before that a few years earlier, when I studied at the League, we saw light and shade, but that was nature. We knew that there was a shadow, but we didn't understand, or I didn't, that that shadow was as valid as the light. Just as valid. We wouldn't see light without shadow. We wouldn't see shadow without the light.

So Hofmann taught Cubism: the push and pull. Positive and negative. Cubism gives you a *block* of space for light. A *block* of space for shadow. Light and shade are in the universe, but the cube transcends and translates nature into a structure.

I felt that the Cubist movement was one of the greatest awarenesses that the human mind has ever come to. Of course, if you read my work, no matter what it is, it still has that stamp. The box is a cube. Now that is very interesting. No matter how original we are, eventually all of us do fall in. In the beginning I just thought my work was such a new world that it even overpowered me as I moved into it. But in time, it has fallen into place.

I have to concede that the time we live in has something to do with our forms. The Egyptians had their forms, the Mexicans, the marvelous Aztec and Mayan had their forms, wherever you go they had the monumental and marvelous, and so they belong of their times. So we do.

Of course, years later, when I went to Spain and saw the architecture and landscape, I recognized that Picasso would have to come from Spain. That landscape was totally Cubistic. More so than any landscape I've seen. And think of the colonial houses where I grew up in Maine. Every room was squared off, and then the whole house was box-shaped. I must say that I was aware, definitely aware, that the great artists must express their early childhood. We've absorbed it, you see. Art is the essence of awareness, and you can't be aware of something out of the blue. You are aware of what you have related to from the earliest recollections. More and more I see the human mind doesn't just spring up . . . we take a great deal from our environment.

LN, 1931, Munich

On that first trip to Europe I stayed in Munich for about three months. Then I did some moving picture work as an extra in Munich and in Vienna. In the spring, probably April, I wanted to see Salzburg before I left for Paris. Now certain places demand certain expressions. In Salzburg the geography of the land contained sound. I got to Salzburg and it was still snowing and I was walking through a mountain pass (I was alone) and that mountain and the passage . . . well, I cannot tell you why, it certainly wasn't conscious, but I began singing . . . S I N G I N G . . . as if I was reaching the top of the mountains. You see, that was a landscape that demanded sound and echo.

On the way back from Germany to the United States, I stopped in Paris for the first time. I stayed at the Hotel Raspail, which means that I went to the Dôme every morning . . . you would meet daily at the Dôme, five cents a cup of coffee. But I'll tell you, Diana, I had already lived a certain way; I already was in a different position. Then I moved to the Rue de Bologne, and also I had met Mr. Wildenstein. So I had the two sides, tasted of the two extremes.

Mr. Wildenstein said that he would like to see the work that I had brought from Hofmann's class and we talked. Then when they opened the big gallery here, they built—see, they had had a place on Fifth Avenue where Baroness Rebay had shown, and then they built that building on 64th Street. So when they opened it, he invited me to the opening. I was still, of course, a student at the time. But he was very wonderful to me.

So here I was, touching, in 1931, top situations. I would say that one thing I never forgot in Paris was the museum of African sculpture—the Musée de l'Homme. I went in and saw, not only the masks, I saw an animal, and I recognized the *energy*. And I think that was a milestone. Because it's true that Picasso had already found African sculpture, but until I went there I had never seen it. So it was the first exposure to that and I recognized the lines and the strength and the power.

That first trip I was anxious to get back to see Mike. The whole time I was in Europe, the guilts and the weights of separation, the weight of leaving Mike, was a great responsibility. I think people should think a million times before they give birth. The guilts of motherhood were the worst guilts in the world for me. They were really insurmountable. You see, you are depriving another human being of so many things, and the other party also knows it. That struggle blinds you. That's the price, the great price.

When I came back to New York, Mike was in Maine with my family. I went to visit him and then I was on my own in New York. But after a few months I decided, with my mother's encouragement, to go back to Paris because I felt I had not seen enough. I pawned my diamond bracelet and went back to really study French art and architecture.

I met Louis-Ferdinand Céline on the boat, the *Liberté*. It was summer and a lot of interesting people were on the ship. It was a small boat, and it was all one class. One dining room. I was with other men and Céline wasn't at my table, but he came over to me and he started to speak. He was a man about . . . well, you wouldn't say tall but you wouldn't say short, about five foot ten or so, and a little bit of a careless dresser. He had rather a big head with blue eyes. *Very nervous.* But I found him very exciting because of all this. Everyone knew who he was. He had finished *Journey to the End of the Night* and had gone to Hollywood with Jean Gabin, the actor (to see about making a movie), but when they found out his political leanings they didn't do anything. I remember that he had books with him, because he autographed a lot and gave some to me. I had them (for years) and eventually I gave them away.

I didn't know too much about his books until later, but he came over and spoke to me, and he spoke of rather serious subjects . . . humanity and the origins of humanity. He was a doctor, and brilliant. He told me about his mother, about the difficulty he had had in getting an education. His mother used to sell patent medicine from house to house so he could go to medical school. I don't know if he even had a father, but he was an only child. And he studied to be a doctor and he became a doctor. Another thing I remember . . . we talked about his appearance and he said, "You know, I'm the end of a line. I'm peasant stock. When you have a head like mine it's the end of a period."

He said he'd like to see me in Paris. He wrote to me from Paris. But I got awfully busy, and I'll tell you, Diana, I wasn't so anxious to see him, because he'd already told me he hated Jews.

The point was, he had it tied up with history. He said that when the world goes under, when it's decadent, the Jews come up. He said it differently, but I *think* that's what he said.

So then when I got to Paris, I was invited out. I already had someone on the boat, and I was pretty conventional at that moment. Later I became different, but this was when I had just left my marriage. But then he wrote letters to New York, and I did see him in New York City several times later. I had a large apartment off Third Avenue on 15th Street, across from the

St malo

21

Dear Miss nevelson,

By now you must have been
married one or one again. What possession
will be left for me.?
  I will be in Paris Saturday Sunday —
  come Have lunch with me any day
  You say — but write one day before.
98 Rue Lepic

  Where is that money?

  Louis FC —

Letter to LN from Louis-Ferdinand Céline in Paris

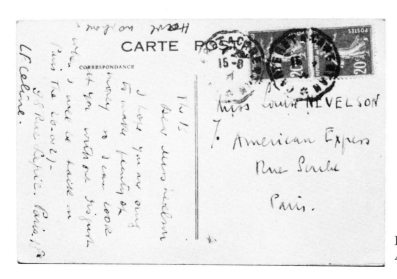

Postcard from Céline.
Archives of American Art

Friends School. Mike was living with me, and that's why I took it. It was near his school and it had studio space. It was awfully tough because I had not made, in 1932, a place for myself. I was in the throes of a bit of despair. And also that was the time I recognized that when I permitted other influences in my life, it didn't work. I think that at that moment, as much as Céline might appeal to me, I wasn't ready.

He came to the house and he was very friendly. We never got intimate or anything, and yet he proposed. He said, how would I like to marry him. This is a funny thing, Diana. Now I know that Céline *saw* me, but I couldn't encourage it. My whole life was built on different lines. I didn't believe in the nature of marriage as such. I had left a marriage to be free. And I wasn't about to marry a man who hated Jews. I said, truly . . . I remember this because I think it could already have appeared in *Life* magazine that he was a Nazi. Later on they had an article on who in France was against France when the Germans invaded, and among them, the spies and things, was Céline. That can be looked up. But the way he spoke, I had already gotten the message, and so I said to him, "You know, dear, you would be worth more dead than alive to me." Well, he didn't contradict that. I think he understood.

What I'm bringing out is that Céline was a total fanatic. And don't you know that fanatics, for instance, if they hate Jews, *love* to marry Jewish women. I also think we haven't yet . . . I haven't, anyway, solved the relationship—the phrase—the battle of the sexes. Now they tell you to love but there's *a constant battle of the sexes*. I think that in the sexual act, as delightful as it can be, the very physical part of it is, yes, a hammering away. So it has a certain brutality. I think that is what the women are really trying to do, to solve that problem. Not to solve it, but to get closer to understanding it. Because even when men have been good to women, well, we're good to our animals, too.

But Céline was a fascinating man. I would always describe him as a fascinating man. Now maybe not to everybody, to me, having lived as I have. Céline at that time was on the point of despair. He wasn't a drinking man as such. He was a thinking man. And his mind was going a million miles a minute, and I felt it and the machinery and it was exciting. He didn't have much respect for humanity. He was a doctor, but he didn't because . . . naturally he was very egocentric, self-centered, but he had read a great deal and I think he was an only child, brought up, as I understand, in poverty. He was *totally* bitter. Nothing on earth would appease him. And that's why I think he might have understood me a little. But he had a deep understanding of humanity. And I don't think it was shyness, but he had a kind of relationship towards me without any of the superficial things.

Now of course if someone like that came to me today, I would have a whole different concept of it and would handle it differently. I think that in certain minds that are ripe, you can really transcend a great deal. And I don't think I would be caught in "oh, this and oh, that." Because truly where I'm sitting today, I cannot use anger as I have. I've removed people, altogether, so far that I'm not involved.

You know, I regret that I didn't keep Céline's letters or the letters of Charles Olson. These two men were men that were conscious of themselves. Let's put it that way. They were conscious of the self, which is fine.

When I got to Paris, I stayed at the Hotel Scribe near the American Express. I went to the Louvre. I went to Chartres and all the cathedrals, Versailles . . . all the museums. That was my objective.

This time in Paris I was freer in a way, mentally. And yet I was discouraged. I was discouraged with friendships and I was up a dead end. Because I thought the second time, I would go freer, I would gain more. Not only gain more, but enjoy it more. Well, I guess the people I met never met my own needs, so that was quite a letdown. You see, I was probably jumping hurdles at such a pace that now, in retrospect, who could keep up to that?

It was on this trip that I wrote some poems: "At sea, at sea, what can it be / That I remained so long at sea." I *was* desperate and I was at sea, because everything seemed to me so disjointed and I wasn't connected with anything and of course, don't forget that was a terrible thing to go through. It seemed that everything I touched was negative, from my point of view. But I think what it did for me was it threw me *back* on myself. It gave me a kind of determination *not* to look too much out, but to build myself. It's a price to pay . . . it was a tough lesson. Everything I did pushed me back into myself for self-survival. And what did I want *self*-survival for? To project what I felt about the way I see the so-called world. But what happened is in time, in my studies of metaphysics which were not really so deep, I had to sort of negate the visual world into a place where *I* projected the world. And slowly what happened through searching was a rebuilding into myself and constantly taking full responsibility for my life. And I think I'm still doing that.

I think I stayed about six weeks. Eventually I went to the Riviera and then I took the boat from Genoa to New York.

*W*hen I came back from Europe in the fall of 1932 I was altogether on my own, and I knew that I would just have to swim or sink. No one was going to swim for me and no one was going to sing for me. The outside world pressures you into a mold, but if you don't accept that—you gamble with life. Call it gambling. You know when I decided to become professional—that means to expose yourself naked to the world with the other creative minds—I said, "I'm going into areas I don't know. I might just fall right down to hell and kill myself." And I said, "Well, who cares? I'd rather do it and see what it's about." I don't want the safe way. The safe way limits you.

I studied again at the Art Students League because Hofmann had come to America and was teaching there. George Grosz was there, so I studied painting with him and I studied drawing and painting with Hofmann. When Hofmann was in Germany, he knew already that Hitler was coming into power, and he was evidently very aware. That's why he wanted to get out. He was not a very well-known artist in Europe. He only became a hero, darling, in this country. After the Second World War, and with the GI Bill he had more students than he could handle. The government paid for them. Then he got a gallery. He got going in New York.

Untitled drawing, pencil on paper, 14″ x 13¼″, by LN, 1932. *Whitney Museum of American Art*

Untitled drawing, pencil on paper, 10¾″ x 11½″, by LN, 1930. *Whitney Museum of American Art*

Untitled drawing, ink on paper, 14⅛″ x 21″, by LN, 1930. *Whitney Museum of American Art*

Untitled drawing, ink on paper, 9″ x 11¼″, by LN, 1932. *Whitney Museum of American Art*

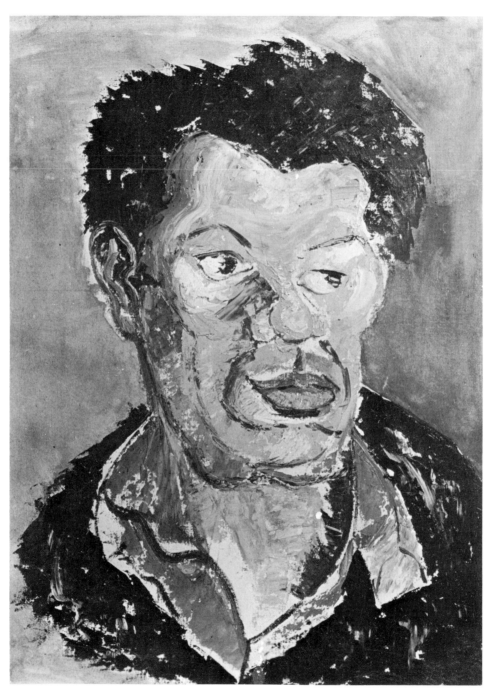

LN's oil painting of Diego Rivera, 16″ x 20″, 1932

Once in class at the League he picked up one of my abstract figures and said to the class, "You see this, this is bigger than life." I had more friends after that day!

I met Marjorie Eaton in Hans Hofmann's class. And she introduced me to Diego Rivera. Diego had come to America to do that big mural for Rockefeller Center, and that was practically finished, so he and his wife Frieda Kahlo moved down to 8 and 10 West 13th Street to do the two smaller murals, one on 14th Street and one a little further up, on 15th Street east. Now Marjorie Eaton had known Diego and Frieda in Mexico, and she was working with him, and consequently she took my drawings to Diego. There was another studio empty in his building, and Marjorie and I took it. So we were all together—for a time: Ellen Kearns had a studio, Diego and Frieda had a studio, and we had a studio. I worked on the small mural on 14th Street. I think it was called *The Workers.*

I knew then, in 1932, where Diego stood. There was grandeur there, honest thinking and generosity, but his feeling for illustration prevailed. I didn't want his imagery even then, so it wasn't a great fight on that level. I had to seek my own way of communicating. But as a human being and as a creative man, he was a great artist. The man was, to my way of thinking, the most giving person.

Their house was always open in the evening, and anyone who wanted to would come. They were very serious about people; they didn't make distinctions. I was never in a home like Diego's. Princesses and Queens . . . one lady richer than God. And workmen, laborers. He made no distinction, and all were treated like one body of people. It was very simple. Diego and Frieda liked it so much because at the other place uptown they had had a doorman, and of course Frieda and he did not believe in that. They were delighted to find a place where they could come in and not be bothered. So every night people came, and then he'd take the gang to a little Italian restaurant on 14th Street.

Frieda was stunning. She wasn't very tall, but she was slender. She was very Mexican-looking, and she wore Mexican clothes and jewelry. Her work was Surrealist. You see, at that time Dali had come right to the front. I think that was when he had a window in Bonwit Teller's. He was at his peak. But Surrealism as Frieda used it could be very much like Mexico—those Santos. They're all surrealistic, whether they know it or not. Of course she did it with a knowingness. Not a message like they, but most of her things *are* messages (in their own way) because they're practically all self-portraits. In different settings.

How she had met Diego—she was only thirteen and she was in Catholic school, private school, and one day he came in, or he may even have taught there, and she told him she would marry him. And she did. It took some time, but she was determined to marry him. She knew what she wanted in life and she was living that life.

You know, if you want to analyze marriage . . . I won't go into analyzing it, but it's some kind of a partnership. Both people feel a certain need. Diego had told me that he loved beautiful women because he always thought of himself, even when he was growing up, as being plain and ugly. I don't think so. He was large and had a great generosity. But you can see that I judge him from one point of view and as a male he would judge himself differently. Now his first wife, Lupe, would come here to New York and stay with them. And she really was a beauty. Now if I say that, it does not diminish Frieda's beauty. She was rather statuesque, and if I remember right, she had sort of hazel eyes and dark hair. She was gorgeous. I don't know whether I think Diego loved these women; he needed them.

Groups followed Diego. He didn't care whether there were a thousand people where he was working—the more the merrier. If we heard that he was going to lecture, he'd have all the art students with him. He was a very sweet man, also couldn't face up to things in his own life, and yet in his public life he was a great fighter. He could get up in public and demolish, say, the Rockefellers in two minutes.

Diego's murals were in the R.C.A. Building and the Rockefellers were going to give them to the city. When he finished the mural he was stopped by the Rockefeller family because it wasn't like the pencil sketch he did. He introduced the head of Lenin in the middle and the Rockefellers didn't like that, but they paid him the full amount of the contract, anyway. Eventually, of course, it was destroyed by the real estate people.

I remember that the Rockefellers paid Diego the five thousand dollars that was agreed upon. And it must have been that Diego had the reputation of giving, because people would know when he had a buck—they'd just smell it. So when he got the five thousand dollars, before we knew it, it had all been given away. There were two entrances to the studio—the one for the guests, and the one for the help. People would ring the bell all day. Well, he never

offended anyone. He would put money in a white envelope and seal it so no
one was offended. And so when it came time for them to leave America for
Mexico by boat, he didn't have any money. We got together a group, put the
money together, and bought tickets for them. Took them bodily onto the boat
and saw that they left.

The first Museum of Modern Art show was in Rockefeller Center in the
Municipal Arts Building, and I was in that show. The artists were selected by
four museum directors of New York City and the show represented all phases
of work from the modern to Academic. I remember I showed a dancing figure
that was later done in bronze. In the beginning I couldn't afford bronze, so I
used Tattistone. Let me tell you what it is. When you carve you have chips
and dust. Well, that dust, more or less you grind that up and then you use a
glue, you make it into a cement. And then you make a mold and you put that
in and then you break your mold. Now that's not new, but the material was
new and you could add colors to it.

Now at that time I did figures that were mostly painted plaster. You asked
before why I painted the sculpture. I was really searching for form. I painted
each plane a different primary color so that the form would be as clear a line
as architecture. That equaled architecture.

Candidly, I've always thought that two dimensions, the flat surface like in
painting, is far superior to sculpture. Now why? Because painting, you have an
illusion. I feel that there's more myth and more mystery in painting—because
you have to give three dimensions to a two-dimensional plane. You look at a
flat surface and you've got your depth—that's an illusion. (When we are giving
up, today, the illusion of space in a picture, that doesn't suit me.) Sculpture's
more physical. Sculpture, we have the four sides, reality. You go around the
piece and you have a whole reality. But a great painter or a great sculptor
transcends it. So we're only talking about the laws. Since we know that
greatness breaks laws.

Of course, I have never *left* two dimensions, because I've always been
doing etchings and lithographs and drawing. I'm drawing all the time. If you
really go through just one piece of mine, you can see drawing. Take two
fingers together and you will see a line between them. Well, that's what gives
these two fingers their definition—just that line . . . and that's just what
makes my work. It's really the line between two objects. You see how delicate
that can be?

Now when I take these old woods that have nails in them or are scratched

Thru A-Z, lithograph, 20″ x 25½″, by LN, 1970. *Whitney Museum of American Art*

Double Imagery III, lithograph, 53¾″ x 42″, by LN, 1967. *Whitney Museum of American Art*

The Clown (holding the world in the palm of his hand), bronze, 12″ square base, 16″ high, by LN, early 1940s. *Jeremiah W. Russell*

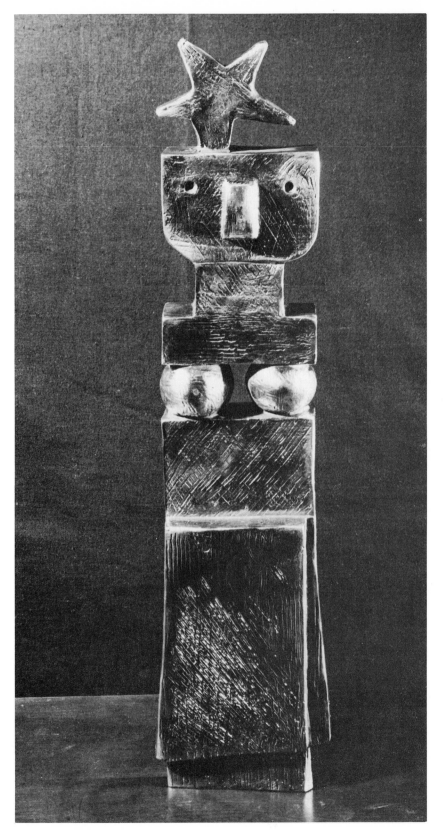

Female Figure with Star, bronze, 21½″ x 5½″, by LN,
early 1940s. *Jeremiah W. Russell*

and have texture, that to me is drawing. Where they're dented—that's a drawing, or where it sucks up space and becomes darker. I don't necessarily plan it that way, very often I find them that way. They have a life of their own. When I put pieces together, that means that I'm applying drawing as well. Every piece is not just a piece, it's a connection. It seems I make all my work *just to draw.*

Without drawing, you wouldn't *do* anything. That's the missing link, really. When you encompass an object, you are making a visual drawing. With your eye you are drawing to define that object. That same line that goes through a pencil or goes through a graphic or oil paint is the same line of consciousness. It's in us. Measurement is in us. Because every time we take a step we're drawing not to fall.

Now for me, in the thirties, sculpture was taking and putting into three dimensions to really see what each side said, what the back said. You can't do it on a flat surface. You're handicapped. It has to be frontal. At that time I felt that once I had form I wouldn't be floundering. And the minute I painted those pieces, you could see clearly the forms. In other words, the definition. I wanted every line to really build into the other.

Basically it's like architecture. The principles have to be valid because it has to stand, and not only physically, but stand on this other level of creation. The fourth dimension is really the place where you give it its principles and form. Most people think there are three dimensions. Now three dimensions is physical, the world of reality, so-called. But I think the Cubists went beyond. Take something like a chair, or a cube. You can only see three sides. Isn't it too bad that our eyes are not X-ray and we can't see around it? You see how limited we are. But knowing that, we assume that a fourth side must be there or it wouldn't stand up. Our eye can never take in that dimension, but the mind does. It's not what you see, it's what you are assuming to *finish* what you are seeing that is, for lack of a better definition, the fourth dimension. Cubism gave us that assumption. And that was a foundation.

It's the equal to what Mary Wigman did at the time with dance. She was the first to go down to the earth center. You see, ballet is this way, against gravity. Everyone was on tiptoes and everyone thought it was beautiful, and it was. She was on the earth and under the earth and people threw tomatoes and whatnot at her . . . but she went back to source. Now, as great as she is, as great as any of us are, you are part of the times. The world had reached these high points and they had left the roots, and in this period, this historic present period where the Cubists came, they took everything and gave it a certain form, like the roots of all.

I met Ellen Kearns through Diego and Frieda. At that time John Flanagan, the sculptor, had a wife who was studying dance with Ellen. He worshiped Diego, so every day he would come and just sit and watch Diego. One evening they asked if they could bring Ellen for dinner, because she was so anxious to meet Diego, and in the same building. So he said sure.

We were all going out and we had a gay time. We used to carry on. We went to a little Italian restaurant on 14th Street in the cellar. There'd be a white tablecloth and we'd put, say, powdered sugar on it. I made a whole composition that went to Diego at the head of the table. Then he'd move around it, and then someone else would get it. We would really compose. Right there. We'd put wine for something, spill that. Then we'd take pepper . . . and we would compose and by the time we left, the tablecloth was a whole landscape. Diego was great for having fun.

Ellen told us that she was teaching modern dance, and she asked me, particularly, if I would come to her dance class. She had been an assistant to Eddy Strawbridge, and he was very famous because he was one of the first to introduce the modern dance company in America. Before that there had been soloists, but not companies as such. Ellen was Eddy Strawbridge's right hand, and she adored him.

She was a good ten years older than I. And it was a contradiction—everything about her physically was wrong for dance. She was fat, the body was all wrong . . . she didn't have one part of the body that was beautiful. But basically she was such an innocent, such a unique person. She had the true spirit of what a nun might have been in the thirteenth or fourteenth century. She had that quality. And here she was teaching modern dance.

So I started and I studied dance with Ellen several times a week, basically evenings, after a day's work. Now this was all new to me, modern dancing and the vitality. And I question whether I'd have had the energy I have without studying with her that we can tap and regenerate our own energy. I think physical activity can be a great source of intelligence. Modern dance certainly makes you aware of movement, and that *moving* from the center of the being is where we generate and create our own energy.

When you know that you're creating, you are aware of all life and not one piece of it. So I felt a body discipline was essential. I studied voice—that uses the body. I studied modern dance which uses the body. I became aware of every fiber, and it freed me. So that if I pick up a cup, or if I put on something—that livingness is all with the same kind of thinking that I put in my work. It takes as much attention. In other words, I wouldn't do anything carelessly. I don't know of a thing that I'm not giving attention to. And I do it as a creative act.

Now Eddy Strawbridge taught modern dance, and Ellen always claimed she didn't teach dance, she taught eurhythmics, the difference being—dance has a form and eurhythmics touches the life force and is freer. It is inner rhythm. If Ellen saw a photograph of a ball player, or Lindbergh, she understood exactly the position, the way he stood, and so on. Now in Germany there was Mary Wigman, who was the first one to get right into the earth. Then there was the Delcore school of eurhythmics in Germany. And Isadora Duncan took Greek things. The Greeks said that you had nine centers of the body (nine muses) that have to open, and the most difficult is the final stage, the opening of the fontanel, the flowering through the head. You see, when a baby is born, the fontanel is open for about the first nine months and then closes, and that is, according to the studies, what has to reopen, so you can imagine how painful, like a metal band around your head. That's the last of the nine centers and the most important. Very few people ever get to that, but Ellen went through the whole thing with Eddy Strawbridge.

I never got to that stage. I didn't get the inner dance as fast as many; I took longer, almost, than anyone. But I had great energy. And I studied with Ellen for a good twenty years or more. I was her right hand for a while. All the students stayed with her for years and years. Many of them could not have come through in their work without her. Ellen had an energy that was unique. And her devotion and her depth of honesty, true honesty, there was such a big dose of it that everyone got it. She was very giving, and she had a lot of power in her quiet way. The interesting thing is that she never could give a dance recital herself, but she helped so many students. There was a great conviction and there wasn't a student that she didn't bring to a higher consciousness. And she gave creative energy to anyone who touched her. She gave totally of herself—there was no reservation.

That was one thing. Then she was a scholar, very serious. She read all her life, and she would go to the movies a lot and reinterpret them according to metaphysical studies. I also studied metaphysics with her. She'd have metaphysics certain evenings. And she herself had a teacher that had taught her metaphysics, so she took me there, too. When you delve into metaphysics, you find there's no difference between the depths of metaphysics and the depths of art. Because they use the same symbols. It is universal. But here's where I was caught. The teachings could be all right, but the teachers themselves abused their powers. Ellen wasn't like that, and that was her great gift. I still think Ellen was one of the most unique people on earth.

I studied with her from the 1930s to the 1950s. And at that time, dance was a vital force. It was like dance was *carrying* America at that time. Martha Graham, by the nature of her spirit, by the nature of her energy, by her presence and intensity, reflected our times. Graham was undoubtedly movement of the twentieth century. She was a pioneer. Now Isadora Duncan, in her great freedom of life, stemmed from the Greek dance. Nevertheless because she came originally from California, which was both pioneer and virginal at that time, she brought a new life to these dance forms. She was like a breath of fresh air. She took the Greek forms and gave them a great, new movement. She was really the first American, to my awareness, that the world recognized. They couldn't help but recognize her, because no matter what she did, *she brought this great, pioneering spirit into movement.* I wish I could say it better because I appreciate her so.

When Isadora Duncan gave her last concert, she was already about fifty-one. Being a great artist, she waited for this beat. Then she didn't quite get it and she didn't dance. But there was one second and she raised her hand, and that was the concert. Now the unknowing people thought she was nuts, and they knew she drank a little, or a lot, and they said, she's old, she's fat, she's drunk. But the great admirers and lovers of true dance said this was the great essence, because she did not have to do more, because in that one movement she had said everything she had to say. It was wonderful. It was great genius. It encompassed her whole conscious creative life at that particular moment. Because she was a great artist she could do it and she knew what she was doing. Somebody else less would have fallen flat on their face.

Now we can say she was *true* to her time. Martha Graham has been *true* to her time. Both of these people are great artists, and you must remember that the setting, the time, the atmosphere was ready for them. When Martha

Graham came on the scene, it was like the earth had been rained on and everything was clear and she was ready.

When there is that kind of depth and creativity, you will find it moving in every area. It takes a whole world of mentality to give us a period. The 1920s and 1930s gave us certain things: the thirties was already beginning to give us depths.

You know, when *Guernica* came to the MOMA, it was a big event. Because when I saw *Guernica*, I really feel that it touched me as much as any creative painting. Now, why? First, the color. Black, gray, white. And then the way he used form. The horses, and what he did with them. How he reconstructed a world. So if you look at it, you realize that the visual universe changed if you looked at that picture. It changed from the point of view of form. It changed the whole world of form. Second, that its content and what it told about humanity was an essence of all times and all places. I had always identified with Cubism from its earliest stages. Cézanne. Now I had seen early Braques and early Picassos, and they were complicated and sophisticated and remarkable. But when I saw *Guernica*, it encompassed a whole totality. So it reaffirmed something to me. That painting could not have been made before. The impact. The *strength* that every line said. If you want to read it you will see that Cubism was necessary to make that statement. I still think, for me, it is one of the great paintings of our times.

Without the WPA I question whether New York would have become the art center of the world. During that period De Kooning was young, Kline, Rothko, all of them . . . Pollock . . . and they were getting this check, doing their work. Models were sent. Also the poets and the writers and the actors and actresses—they were all on the project. So there were these many cultural advantages. Without that project, I question whether the De Koonings and the Gorkys and the Klines and Rothkos would have survived. Only after that did we begin to see these people flourish.

I knew Gorky well in the early thirties, when I came back from studying in Europe. He was the poorest of all. He didn't have any money, and he used to eat spaghetti every day for weeks. He had this studio on 16th Street, and I used to go there. Gorky was a tall, tall man with a heavy black moustache. He was a very pious man. He came from the Georgian country in Russia. He was going to be an engineer and then he fell in love with art. His approach to art was with reverence. Art was everything. He was a Cubist, and then he got friendly with Matta who was a Surrealist. And so he introduced that into his paintings. Gorky was a great technician and a very good artist, but he wasn't an innovator. Beautiful color and great refinement.

I remember I was in the Waldorf Cafeteria in the late thirties. There were several men and myself and Mike was with me. We were talking about sculpture. This Greek sculptor . . . he painted his things. They were talking very seriously about art, particularly sculpture, and they said to me, "You know, Louise, you've got to have *balls* to be a sculptor." And that's when I said, "I *do* have balls." So I knew then that nothing like that was going to stand in my way.

No one has a monopoly on creativity. I never recognized that whoever created humans gave a brain only to one sex or the other. I never recognized that distinction. It seems to me that I was just quite sure that I was born this way and I wanted to live my life as I understood it. I was so *absorbed* into what I was doing, the creative problems, that *at the time* I wasn't so aware of that kind of prejudice.

But I'm thinking about the women that are fighting so desperately now, and I have the greatest respect for them. If they're not given an opportunity, we know that they're going to take it now, and nothing will stop them. And rightly so. I hope they do. I think that you have to look into yourself and do what you feel is your fulfillment. If women have not taken their rightful places, they were in a world that was male-oriented and it wasn't ladylike. They were taught to look pretty and throw little handkerchiefs around but never to show that they had what it takes. Well, I didn't recognize that, and I never never played that role. If you play that role, you don't build an empire. But if you want to look in history, we have a lot of women who have built empires.

Now I feel that a woman's work will always be a little different than a man's. There's always a difference in the thinking between male and female. When women are women artists and don't try to ape men, I see a great difference. I feel that through nature I'm totally female, in that sense. Of course, we know that females have male genes and vice versa. But I mean . . . that my whole mind. And then the work that I do is feminine. When I work, I don't work like males. I have never used a ruler to make one piece in my life. It's too mechanical for me. Then I use a scissors to cut certain thin woods. No male would do that. Now, most people feel that because of the abundance of work . . . and it's rather monumental . . . they would like to say, you work like a man. Well, that isn't true at all. That's a preconceived idea.

I think that if a woman is gifted and she's attractive she's going to have a great time on earth. Why would she want to be anything else? I don't think of myself as a strong woman. I never even heard that word about me until recently. I always thought bluntly that I was a glamorous goddamn exciting woman. I didn't want to be strong at anything. I wanted to have a ball on earth. But I wanted it through the channels that I want.

I don't think that anyone that knew me in the beginning ever suspected that I would be the one to arrive at certain things. They didn't because we're camouflaged.

I could have played the role of the down-and-out artist, but I wanted to have fun, and not only fun, I think I fed on it. It was exciting. I always used to dress with a flair. And I liked to swear and I liked to drink and have romances. Well, little did they think that I'd be the one to arrive. *I* knew it, though. I was very sure of what I was doing. I believed in myself and I was utterly satisfied with what I believed in. I wasn't going to let a soul on earth judge my life. But the world has a cliché: I'm from Missouri, show me. I was living in a loft at that time, and not a fancy one like in SoHo. They saw that I dressed well and looked right and everything, and they'd think something was wrong if they saw that I had to live this way. So the great contradiction—who are the judges? The people that live on another level. It always made a problem for me.

Now, why didn't I live with the artists? Well, I did in a way, but that didn't solve it. When I was very young and I first came to New York, it was very fancy to say that you were bohemian. But I saw bohemian meant that you were enslaved in another way. Or to live in the Village—you were part of another group, so I didn't like that. The world, living in the world was a social problem. You see, a person has a potential. Some are gifted, but there is a society. And so you're caught in all the stupidities of that society.

I'd rather work twenty-four hours a day in my studio and come in here and fall down on the bed than do anything I know. Because this is living. It's like pure water; it's living. The essence of living is in doing, and in doing, I have made my world and it's a much better world than I ever saw outside.

*I*n the late thirties I was in a studio on Bleecker Street, not for very long. While I was living there, I had to go to a dental clinic and the head of it was a young man with red hair. He was very quiet and very intelligent. And he was very gentle and every time I'd go out, he'd come to the door and he began asking if he could visit me. And I said no, because Mike was with me, but I said as summer comes he would probably go to Maine, and I'd be glad to see him and so he said fine. And so we waited.

I was looking forward to it, because I had great respect for him and his abilities. Certainly I wasn't thinking of anything too serious, but it was a nice thing.

So after Mike went away for the summer I called him and invited him over. I expected a fine relationship and, to my great amazement, he kind of threw me on the couch. Nothing happened because I was so *shocked*. He saw it in my eyes. I was *utterly* shocked. So he got angry and left.

And after he left I lay down in bed . . . and I was so shocked that I heard a bird doing this [scratch] and we had a cat, and the cat . . . and I heard the cat attack the bird. I was in such shock, suspended animation, that I couldn't open my eyes. I couldn't confront it. I knew what was happening. I knew that the cat had attacked the bird and I couldn't take it any longer. So I looked in my purse and I had a couple of dollars, maybe three, and I had seen in the paper that *Hi-Tor*, by Sherwood Anderson, was playing—that's when Burgess Meredith became a great star. It said, "Last day." It must have been on a Saturday. And so, I was alone and I thought, I can't take it. I'm going to leave this place.

I get on a bus, and go to the theater, take a ticket, and I go in. It must have been evening. So I'm standing. It's the last night. The usher later came and said, "You can sit in that seat behind a post," and so I sat down. And the play was set in the past and was about a ship that sank with all its passengers aboard. Now *Hi-Tor* (I didn't know it really existed until lately) is a mountain—high, and overlooking the Hudson River. So that Burgess Meredith was standing way up sort of in a shack and read the list of the names of the passengers below and each one came forward and told their history. They were "dead" so that they walked off-balance on the stage in these period costumes and their voices came from a distance like echoes.

Well, that's all I needed. And it took me back into death and metaphysics, and I thought, did I have to attract that? I didn't know what the play was going to be about. All I knew was that it was the hit of the season. Well, I just thought it was the end. It meant that I was attracting the bird with the cat and I came here and there was death. Drowned. The ship went down . . . I was in a terrible state. When I went home I knew that that cat had killed the bird and I began cleaning, and sure enough, behind the bookcases, I found the dead bird.

But I had led up to this because it was cold . . . there were too many rooms. We had gas but you couldn't really get heat and it was the worst time somehow, because I was living in a state of graveyards. I saw graveyards with fire. There was death, again symbolic, and I needed heat so much, I saw fire. And I'd go to bed every night like that. I knew, in some way, as bad as the other was in Paris, that was one state but this was the other. The other was a bit of reality, and disappointment. But this was total death. So that was a bad state, but the funny thing was I was doing a lot of sculpture.

I think most artists create out of despair. You know, when you're pregnant, there are the physical pains of labor in nature. But if labor pain is for physical birth, then there is a psychic pain and spiritual for creation.

Through the periods of creation over the years I have had these deep psychic depressions. I've often questioned—if I had had help or had met a different circumstance—whether I could have—I don't want to say made my life easier, I want to say whether I could have avoided these great despairs. I don't know. Because I certainly entertained suicide. But I had this child and I was a parent and I just couldn't let anyone down. I certainly wanted to. Under different circumstances, with the feeling I had, I don't think I could have confronted these sharp exhaustions. But I will say that after I come out of these experiences, I am more sensitized. Not while I'm going through them. I wouldn't have chosen these psychic labor pains at all. But since I had them, it seems to me I would not have unfolded to this point without them. When I began to have big exhibitions it was always felt there was a mystic quality, and I think that is what it might have given me—a kind of depth.

I did consult a very celebrated analyst about fifteen years ago, because I had problems with the young man who was working with me that I wanted to straighten out. So I thought as long as I was coming to him I would like to look into my own life, so as to get a greater insight. And this analyst said, "Mrs. Nevelson, you are the most masochistic person I have ever met."

So I said, "How do you account for my arriving in the art world to the degree I have, if I'm that masochistic?" And he said, "Well, you've done it in spite of yourself." Now, of course I can't quite agree with that statement. The nature of creation is that you have to go inside and dig out. The very nature of creation is not a performing glory on the outside, it's a painful, difficult search within.

So the thirties was very difficult. The whole country was in a state of despair after the Crash. My own family suffered financial reverses, too—that was the Hoover time when they sold apples on the street.

In the toughest economic days, I didn't have the price to go uptown. The WPA did give us a little breathing space. I only came in on the tail end, in 1937 when it was almost over. You had to get on relief to get on the project, and I didn't quite want to fill out the papers because my family were helping me at the time, but by 1937, I felt it was necessary. So I taught on the project, but I also did painting and sculpture. You could go and learn how to cast and learn about patina, and I did. All my sculpture I had in my first show at Nierendorf in 1941 I did right on the project.

I trained myself not to waste. I feel that if you know you're going to live your life as an artist, you steel yourself daily. You don't develop fancy tastes, fancy appetites. An artist once said to me, "Well, it's all right, Mrs. Nevelson, but I have to eat." And it offended me. And I said, "Who said you have to eat?" You know you can eat bread or a cup of tea or a can of sardines when you're hungry. As a matter of fact, I prefer that to most of the fancy restaurants in New York. I couldn't afford to get caught in a lot of things on earth, because I had my sights in another place.

Now I had met this Italian doctor who was a skin specialist. He had come to New York during World War II. A very sporty type who had traveled in society and on the Riviera and he didn't react to me, at all. I went uptown with my sister Lillian, and while she was in the doctor's office, I waited in a nearby drugstore on the corner of 57th and Lexington and had a cup of coffee. It was pouring with rain outside, very gloomy. I was working on my sculpture and had paint on my hands and face. My hair was wet and I was drenched. I was a mess. And in walks the doctor. It was about quarter to three and at three o'clock he went to the hospital. All of a sudden, he took notice of me and began telling me how exciting I was. The reverse of his first reaction to me. He said, "What can I *do* for you! What can I *give* you." And he carried on. Well, here I was. A five-cent cup of coffee looked good. And there were no finances, nothing. I said, in all seriousness, because of the way I lived . . . it seemed that something GRAND should happen. I said, "You can send me some black orchids, with a mirror at the bottom of the box, so that they will be multiplied." He said, "I'll send them to you tomorrow morning."

The next morning I waited for the orchids. And I waited and waited.

LN, early 1940s

Finally I called my sister and said, "You know I didn't get the orchids!" She started to laugh and said, "After all, Louise, what did you expect? It was just talk." But by then, I was very serious about the whole thing. It was a promise, as I saw it. And I was very disappointed. I was probably more than disappointed. I didn't quite need the orchids, I must say. But I wanted them. It seemed like a bouquet, and a great luxury. Sure enough, by noon, I got the orchids. With a great big beautiful mirror at the bottom. The orchids were dark brown, really, and they were gorgeous. And it seemed like a wish fulfilled. A fulfillment of a realization. A recognition.

*A*t that time I was so desperate that I decided—like I always decide my own destiny, I guess—that I had to have a show or I was going to cut my throat. I'd been out with a distant relative of mine, and I think he must have spent a great deal of money, maybe a thousand dollars for the day. We lived it up. The shock of extravagance and the contrast with my situation was so great that—I was at the Plaza at the time and we had lunch and I walked out of there and I said to myself, what's the best gallery in New York? Well, I'm going in there and if I don't get a show, I'll shoot him. So I walked over from the Plaza to the Nierendorf Gallery.

Now Nierendorf was considered at that time to be the best gallery in New York for modern art. He was the one who brought and introduced Paul Klee to this country. He had Picassos, he had all of those European artists. His gallery was on the south side of 57th Street, between Madison and Fifth. Number 18 East 57th Street. So I went in there and I introduced myself. And he said, "What can I do for you?" And I said, "I want an exhibition in your gallery, Mr. Nierendorf."

And I guess he thought something was a little strange. So he said, "But I don't know your work." And I said, "Well, you can come and see my work." He said, "Where do you live?"

At that time I had a little place on 21st Street. When the WPA closed about six months before, they had taken all the sculpture and broken it up and thrown it in the East River. But the man who was in charge asked me if I wanted my work returned, and I said yes. And so I had it in the cellar. So Nierendorf came the next evening, looked at the pieces, and said, "You can have a show in three weeks."

I think we create our lives. I'm not going to accept words like *luck* and *break*, none of it. First, I wouldn't permit it. I don't want breaks. I don't want the outside to superimpose. In my structural mind, I couldn't afford it—"luck." If others think that way, I feel a weakness in their structure of thinking.

So we had the show, and it was received very well by the critics. And Nierendorf was pleased. Nevertheless, there were no sales. I had moved from the house on 21st Street to an enormous loft on East 10th Street, alone in a four-story building. Fifteen dollars a month. It was cold and I was miserable and I just lay in bed. And I saw *darkness* for weeks. It never dawned on me that I could come out of it, but you heal. Nature heals you, and you do come out of it. All of a sudden I saw a crack of light . . . then all of a sudden I saw another crack of light. Then I saw *forms* in the light. And I recognized that there was no darkness, that in darkness there'll always be light.

But still I was alone and struggling. And I was emotionally caught in war, that's violence, caught in guilt. Mike was in the war, at sea with the Merchant Marines. When he went to Egypt or Russia and it was secret, they couldn't inform us, and six months at a time I didn't hear from him. It threw me into a great state of despair. And I recall that my work was black and it was all enclosed—all enclosed. I couldn't think of doing a piece in the round.

I would use black velvet and close the boxes. In other words, this was a place of great secrecy within myself. I didn't even realize the motivation of it; it was all subconscious, it was the expression of a mood. But it isn't only *one son.* It's also that the *world* was at war and *every* son was at war. And it was an atmosphere in the world, right through the world. I evidently live so much *in* the world and *out* of the world, both places, that I was right in the middle of it. And I thought at the time that I would *never* have a piece of work in the open again.

I didn't make sculpture to share my experience. I was doing it for myself. I did it because I knew I was in a spot, and I had to move out of it to survive. Almost everything I had done was to understand this universe, to see the world clearer. I think that ultimately what drove me so desperately was . . . I could only understand through working. That means, through myself.

That was when I began using found objects. I had all this wood lying around and I began to move it around, I began to compose. Anywhere I found wood, I took it home and started working with it. It might be on the streets, it might be from furniture factories. Friends might bring me wood. It really didn't matter.

Mike in Egypt during the war

Now, no one, to my knowledge, at that time was using old wood. Sculptors were using the torch. It somehow wasn't what I wanted. The noise and the masquerade offended me, and I didn't like the execution. It was too mechanical for me. Because I was creating every second, with this great intensity and great energy. And I just automatically went to wood. I wanted a medium that was immediate. Wood was the thing that I could communicate with almost spontaneously and get what I was looking for. For me, I think the textures and the livingness . . . when I'm working with wood, it's very alive. It has a life of its own. If this wood wasn't alive, it would be dust. It would disintegrate to nothing. The fact that it's wood means it has another life.

I remember one thing I saw in Maine, when I came back from Europe the first time. Across from where we were in Monhegan was another island. It was a government island which means if you were on it you didn't have to pay taxes. So I took a boat and went over there, because I saw a group of shacks. This man lived there with sheep and was a recluse, only once in a while he'd go off the island for a chess tournament. But he'd lived there for years. Now wood drifts . . . and he took driftwood and he built one shack. Then he built another shack and then more shacks. He never painted them, so he had the different color wood that he found. You'd see it at a distance and it was rock, like browns, and then the buildings. The architecture was no architecture, the shacks were different sizes, but the whole concept and the combination was very exciting to me. I looked at it and I thought, well, this appeals to me more than neoclassic, because they were so aware and this man did it through need, but it became a whole environment.

Another thing that fascinated me and really clicked it for me—I was living on East 10th Street and I'd walk up Second or Third Avenue, past the antique shops. And at that time, in the early forties, I didn't have too much in my pockets. Well, in one of these places I saw a paddle, a canoe paddle. It must have been African or Indian—carved. Now, the paddle was thin. It couldn't have been more than a quarter of an inch in depth and probably six inches in width, and it went right up and with the handle and all it was at least six feet long. And the slenderness of it and the glory of it and the love that whoever had handled it gave it, just oozed out of it. I thought that it was unique in its proportion, which encompassed grandeur. And I thought, well, that's a work of art. You see, it was wood, and . . . somehow it touched me.

I thought, well, I'll go in and inquire about this paddle. So I did, and of course even then it was three hundred fifty dollars. That did seem quite a bit

for a paddle. I don't say it wasn't worth it. And today if I was so moved, I would have taken it. But at that time, I just couldn't find a way of getting it.

I've said before that as many times as I've looked in Tiffany's window, or Cartier's, I've really never been moved. Not by the design. According to my way of thinking there's never been a designer who knows how to handle those precious stones. That goes through the ages. They just don't know how to design for them. Now, a diamond—I don't say now that I'm authoritative . . . I am saying it's a transparent, icy piece of nature. That's what it is. And it comes from coal mines. But when you realize the element of time and all to bring it to that place, then it should be treated like, not only a stone, but a kind of genius. I know that genius applies to *people*, but the stone—that is NATURE-GENIUS. To my knowledge there has never been a mind that comprehended its truth or mystery.

Now, you'll say, "Are you in love with a diamond?" No, I'm not in love with a diamond—I think I *understand* a diamond. I appreciate it. So of course there is a great feeling for it. But that paddle that went through some human mind and feeling, consciously or not, had *more* to say to me. You'll notice how consistent it is that I identify with what went through another human mind more than with nature. Nature is a great organized thing, an intelligence in itself. But when that's filtered through the human mind, it becomes another thing. I identify with one, but I work a little bit more through the other. Of course, we have lived with wood through the ages: the furniture in the house, the floors of the houses. There was a time before cement when the sidewalks were made of wood. Maybe my eye has a great memory of many centuries. And maybe there's something about wood that is closer to the feminine, too.

When people grow up and become sophisticated, they want golds and diamonds. When you give them old wood, that doesn't at first represent their status symbol. But fortunately, in our times, we have a great audience in the world who have put away these things, they have seen through them, and then they really come into this and say, "There is no difference." Man through the ages has made different values and stamped them—that does not make them authentic. For example, money, the paper dollar, in itself isn't worth anything, is it? We have made an *agreement* at this point in time that we give it that value, you see, and that goes for many things. I can take a piece of coal, just a plain black piece of coal, and it can be just as beautiful as a diamond. It doesn't have the material value on the market, that's all. But most people judge for the value of what it's worth.

Now you go to the hardware store and buy a dowel. You buy it for a few pennies. Yet that dowel has the same importance in the ultimate scheme of things as a diamond ever did. Oh, the greatest diamond is beautiful and it comes out of the same aliveness and livingness but it doesn't have the same function, it doesn't have a use for me. I tell you when I use that dowel and *place* it, then that order is a rightness in the universe.

To me, actually, some of the poorest and cheapest woods are really the most exciting—the Japanese boxes and crates have the most texture, and they have knots in them. It doesn't matter. During the war there was a shortage of materials, and I decided that creativity was the important thing and I would see things that I could use, everywhere. I always wanted to show the world that art is everywhere, except it has to pass through a creative mind. I had always, way back years ago, felt *that* . . . In my environment as a child I was very aware of relationships. The injustices of relationships. And I suppose I transferred that awareness to material, what we call "inanimate." I began to see things, almost anything along the street, as art. I don't think you can touch a thing that cannot be rehabilitated into another life. And once I gave the whole world life in that sense, I could use anything.

I feel that what people call by the word *scavenger* is really a resurrection. You're taking a discarded, beat-up piece that was no use to anyone and you place it in a position where it goes to beautiful places: museums, libraries, universities, big private houses . . . These pieces of old wood have a history and drama that to me is—well, it's like taking someone who has been in the gutter on the Bowery for years, neglected and overlooked. And someone comes along who sees how to take these beings and transform them into total being.

Now, just think of certain backs of chairs. They're carved, and the wood that was used, the instruments that created it . . . it's almost like surgery. What it has gone through, the life it's had! The parts that have been broken, the nails in it. Every dent in it—the music that gave it sound while hammering. Some bangs were soft, some were loud, and some sounded as if they really hurt. If you really identify with this . . . it has the same human quality we do. We're not that far removed. It grows and moves and if you take a hammer and nail . . . if you want to experiment . . . some of it screams back, and some is quieter. It depends on your awareness of what kind of nail. When we use nails, we use them like music, because the wood has sound, and when it screams it means that nail does not fit that wood.

If it were understood . . . when you do things this way, you are really
bringing them to life. You know that you nursed them and you enhance them,
you tap them and you hammer them, and you know you have given them an
ultimate life, a spiritual life that surpasses the life they were created for. That
lonely, lowly object is not used any more for what it was—a useful object. It
becomes a work of art. It transcends the third dimension and it too arrives
beyond. It takes part in a great creative act *after* practically becoming ashes.
So naturally when I think of daily living there's no room for sentiment—no
room for stupidity—there's no time for any of that. There's total confrontation
with super life.

Now my garage is full of black wood. This is what I call my stock, my raw
materials. The material I use has nothing to do with association and origin.
Most people identify as we have been taught to label things. They'll say, oh,
that's a hat form; oh, that's a panel; oh, that's a piece of chair. But really a
creative mind is virginal and projects into another realm, where we look at it
as if we've never seen it. All objects are retranslated—that's the magic. It's a
translation and a transformation, both.

When I pick up a piece to put *in* a piece, it's living and waiting for that
piece. You don't just *break a thing* and put it in. That becomes self-conscious,
and that has no life. That's why I pick up old wood that had a life, that cars
have gone over and the nails have been crushed. You have to cut it sometimes,
you might even break it sometimes, but it has to be done a certain way, not
broken unconsciously.

So when I begin composing, I have it lying around and I know which
piece to pick with which other piece. Now every piece that you touch and you
look at has a different grain, according to what kind of wood it is; a different
age. And you can't just put woods together. You must put them like . . . they
have to be related, just like human beings. Where we come in is our
recognition. There's an extra sense for that. Some pieces of wood I won't pick
out at all. And then some woods I've had for many years and I knew they were
exciting things, and I couldn't quite place them. It's like people on earth that
are misplaced and all of a sudden they become geniuses. Why weren't they
geniuses the year before? They weren't in the right atmosphere and the right
combination. That doesn't mean they didn't have it. They just had to wait for
their own time. And certainly I've had all the patience in the world with
things like this, whereas in other ways, I've had no patience.

Painted wooden pieces by LN in Helena Simkovitch's garden, early 1950s. *Jeremiah W. Russell*

Illumination—Dark, bronze, 108½″ x 125″, by LN, 1961. *Whitney Museum of American Art*

Different people have different memories, too. Some have memories for words, some for action—mine happens to be for form. Basically, my memory is for wood, which gives a certain kind of form—it isn't too hard and it isn't too soft. Just to show you my relationship with wood, I was having a guest exhibition—this was in the 1950s—and the dealer called me with great excitement and anger. He had a photograph and he said, "You know, Nevelson, there is one piece of this sculpture that is missing." The problem was that a museum wanted to buy the piece—a City-Scape—and I had made it years before I had exhibited it. In time my sense of space had changed—in other words, the so-called negative space certainly became as important as the forms—and there was one piece of wood that I had taken off. Time had given me two versions of this piece. When this museum director wanted the first version, I felt it was justified, since it was dated at the time it was made. So I said to the dealer, "All right, I'll be up in a taxi with the piece within an hour."

Now I had in my other house [30th Street] a kitchen bigger than this and a garden, and I bet I had easily fifty thousand pieces of wood, piled on the kitchen floor. And I didn't count how many pieces I had in the studio, but the studio was loaded. And to my amazement, that piece appeared almost immediately. In two minutes I went and found it, took a taxi, took it up, and put it back on, and the piece went to the museum.

So each individual has awareness for the things they truly identify with. Identification is love. What is love? Love is recognition. When you love, you're so close with it, it's a oneness. You see, when I started in old woods, I had a confidence. I had a confidence that they were right. In other words, I feel in my being that I'm right for what I do. I feel related.

*N*ierendorf told me in the early forties, "Mrs. Nevelson, you must not stay in America. This is a young country and a primitive country. You have the kind of mind that needs an older civilization." I was born in Russia, brought up of course in America, but the thing is, he already felt that I was a sort of Surrealist.

Now I did not care for Surrealism as such at the time, because I felt it was too literary. If you were to ask me how I relate to it I would say that I'm more of a visual abstract surrealist. Do you see the difference? I use it from another dimension. But in America, particularly, not only weren't the people ready for it but I might also say that the museums and curators and directors weren't ready. So Nierendorf said to me, "You should go to Paris, where you will have more civilized, developed people." I said, "Why do you say that?" and we began talking. He said, "Well, it's primitive and you will have a great struggle in America." And now you listen how important this was to me. I said, "But Mr. Nierendorf, this is a young country, and this is a pioneer country, and I feel in my being that I'm a part of this. I was brought up here and I want to be a part of it, of developing this country." And so it was the harder way to do it, of course, but that was the way I felt, and I stayed.

So what I want to tell you is that history played into my life, which I wouldn't have conceded to at the time. New York was becoming the art center. It took many things to permit a flourishing of modern art in America: it took the WPA, it took the Second World War. Nierendorf and Buchholz were anti-Nazi and they came. And Hofmann was anti-Nazi and he came. We got in a way the best of many roots. You know when Peggy Guggenheim came back, she was very fortunate because it was during the occupation in France. You couldn't take things out. But she rolled her things and brought them here. She brought with her Max Ernst. She brought Breton. Later Mondrian, from London. And she got Kiesler to build that museum on 57th Street for her—Art of This Century. And when she started the gallery she put in the things she brought from Europe, and then in the meantime along the way, she married Ernst.

So the war brought these people to our shores, all these creative minds. And under the circumstances, given the times . . . you know, Kenneth Hayes Miller felt that great art could only come from a person that came from that particular country. He felt that if a European came here, he could never really give us the feeling of this country. Well, I don't believe that. I think in our time you recognize that it really is one world. These people came and they gave it to us on a silver platter, and just when we needed it. We were seeing with the eye things we hadn't seen, and so it sharpened our perspective and consequently the whole thing had a great impact on us.

It is only of late that I am allowing that environment, time, space, all have played a part. I feel that I'm willing to recognize another dimension in myself. I would call it a deeper dimension, digging into another level. No one on earth is that original. No matter how individual we humans are, we are a composite of everything we are aware of. We are the mirror of our times. Because even if we don't imitate, say in art, other people, what we have seen and what we have read, what takes place is *bound* to come through. You get it through books, you get it through the air . . . no one is in a shell all by themselves. We all take. Even a man like Einstein took certain principles before he moved on. Whatever we are we breathe the air of the present, you see.

During the time that Peggy Guggenheim came to New York in the forties and came with these people, it was almost like you were breathing the air of Surrealism. I must say that Peggy Guggenheim's role has not been defined. She played a very important role, I think maybe the most important role here, at that time. Because she opened that wonderful museum, which was quite refreshing and a revelation to New York. And she did give shows to new artists. She was sort of a pioneer. She gave Pollock his first show. She gave Rothko a show. She gave Cornell a show. And the fact that she had a women's show was remarkable.

Peggy Guggenheim really gave this museum of hers a great deal of attention. She went there every morning and she sat at the desk and sold the tickets. She really did work and then, while she was in America, also evenings, she would have different artists who were coming from abroad, different lectures. I only remember going to one or two. She would have the elite of the people that were interested in art.

I told you about a party I had after I moved to 30th Street and Peggy was there with Kiesler, among the guests. And there was an opening at the Met. And they said, let's go, let's go. And Peggy said that there was nothing in the Met she wanted to see, because at that time, there was nothing of modern art. Her mother used to take her all the time to museums in Europe, so she had gone through all that. And for her it wasn't "living." I can see what she meant. She was one of the few, really, of that class, that worked through into contemporary art. Because she opened, long before she came here, the first modern gallery in London.

So that has been her life force. She's been fortunate because the artists she's represented were living, so that was a direct communication. She's unique in that way.

Her house was on the southeast corner of East 51st Street, right on the East River. Don't forget that that section, then, goes right into Beekman Place. And it was an old house. It was stucco with a mural on the building, which was rare at the time. And so that house was very lovely. It wasn't that big, in a sense. But the living room was two stories and the furnishings that she had were very special. I don't mean that they were period pieces or unique in that sense. She was already married and living with Ernst. And Ernst loved everything American Indian. He had these big marvelous dolls, Kachina dolls, old ones. And then they had this wonderful horse, like the ones on the carrousels, and it was spirited. And then I remember a great big chair. And that chair, "the throne," he gave later to Duchamp. As a matter of fact, Diana, we saw it at Teeny Duchamp's not too long ago in France. That's the chair. Well, we've traced it now.

Now in her bedroom, there was a form. A dressmaker's form and she had loads of earrings, many pairs, pinned on this form. And she'd take them off to wear them, then she'd put them back.

Curt Valentine came from Cologne, like Nierendorf. He was right where Arnold Glimcher [Pace Gallery] is now. Now Buchholz, if I remember correctly, was sent by the Valentine Gallery in Cologne, and he eventually took over the gallery opposite Nierendorf. Marion Willard was one of the prominent galleries at that time. Don't forget, Marion was a great lover of Paul Klee. And so she, when she opened a gallery, was showing Klee. Then Ralph Rosenborg and Lou Shanker as painters and David Smith as a sculptor. David Smith and Ralph Rosenborg were friends, and they both showed with Marion Willard and later Marion Willard and Buchholz jointly gave David Smith his first big show.

When I saw David Smith's first show, it was Cubistic. Now, I thought that that was a great show. Great strength. Great simplicity. You see, the Cubist. Then it was metal—bronze, an expensive show. And of course he went into the line. Which is another important break. Because the cube is solid and this took it out of it, like drawing. So he was concerned with space in another way. Of course Calder, if you look at the little figures out of wire, was totally drawing. But each one was strong in his own right.

No one on earth has the touch of Ralph Rosenborg. He's probably one of the most unique persons in a visual way. He and David Smith in 1942 came to my exhibition at Nierendorf's and I met Ralph and he took me home to East 10th Street. So Ralph never left and he got busy and showed me how to do dowels. Ralph adored Eilshemius's paintings and we made the frames for them together on 30th Street. He was the one who found that house for me on 30th Street.

I met Mondrian many times, because he came about the time Peggy Guggenheim started Art of This Century, and of course he, for some time, was with that group. I met him through Jimmy Ernst and Elinor Lust. Mondrian loved Jimmy, he was like a father to Jimmy, so he used to go up there. I showed with Elinor, I don't quite remember the year, and so Elinor would have parties and I ran into him all the time. We used to go out dancing. Maybe to Harlem. He loved to dance. He was a wonderful man.

I visited Mondrian in his studio when he was on 59th Street, and it was very simple. Very clean and orderly. So I asked him once, he having lived such an austere life and looking it . . . I said to him, "Did you always live like this? Did you never want beautiful Oriental rugs or things like that?" He said when he was younger he did have those things, but as he got older he simplified. Of course, being Dutch—clean, and so on. He represented his background. But then you have a man like De Kooning who was the reverse. Sometimes you reject a thing, sometimes you accept a thing. I think Mondrian probably *cleaned* everything, even in life, and emotion and all. He lived totally alone. You see what he did, he measured his emotion just as he would make a painting.

This story was told in Nierendorf's gallery. Years ago they *did* a few things. There was a gallery like Julian Levy. They'd have vignettes and lectures, very smart in New York. We don't have that now. It was the American Abstract group, one of the first groups before the Federation even. G. K. Morris gave the lecture, and he said that he had just come from London. He had traveled all around and then he went to London and visited Mondrian, and he went in and they talked, and Mondrian said he disliked his studio so much. He couldn't stand it. And Morris said, "Why?" And he said, "Everything is fine but these round pillars that hold up the fireplace." It offended him every time he looked at it. He had to *do* something about them. And when G. K. Morris traveled to America and then came back to London, he visited Mondrian again and saw those columns. And Mondrian didn't say anything. So Morris said, "What about the columns . . . ?" And Mondrian said, "Oh, I decided to ignore them."

I never met Brancusi. But there was a wonderful story about him coming into Romany Marie's restaurant. He went into the kitchen and saw the butcher block with a large steak on it. He threw the steak against the wall with

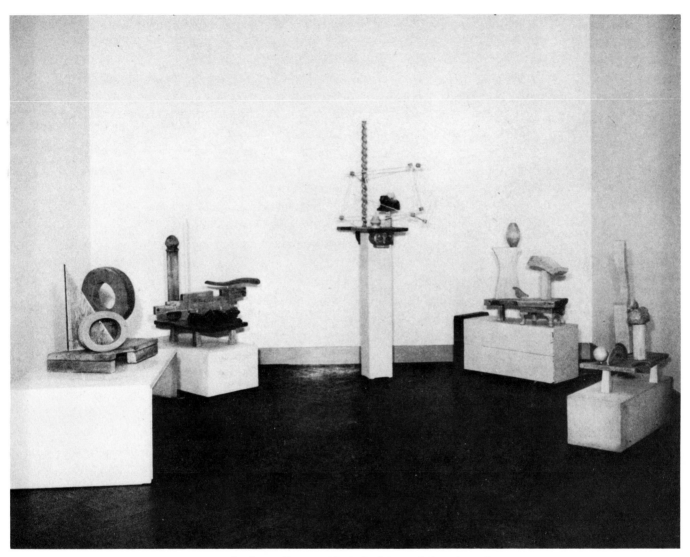

Nierendorf installation, 1944. *Archives of American Art*

great ferocity and said, "I'm going home. I've seen enough of America. I saw what I need to see." And he took the butcher block and got back on the boat to France. He brought the most prized possession in America back with him, according to his dimension.

The thing that is a landmark in my own life is that . . . on one November day, when I was going to the Metropolitan from 10th Street east, I saw this yellow object in a gray atmosphere with snowflakes. It was in November, near Thanksgiving, because I recall the suit I wore and I recall it began just snowing a bit. And there wasn't a bit of sun. Can you see the snow almost coming down, not heavily but it looked like the city was gray-opaque? And so every bit of snow that was coming down, every flake had its prominence. And so under those circumstances, everything was like silhouette.

So, I walked to Wanamaker's, then, and at the corner, I see yellow . . . I see a man walking towards me with a yellow box. And it's so yellow that it makes everything recede . . . The man was walking with this shoeshine box under his arm. And that was the only thing I saw in this gray day. So I walked a few more steps, and I turned around and ran after this man. I was moved. I couldn't let him go. I took a few steps back and ran and chased him. I stopped the man and said, "You have a beautiful shoeshine box." I asked him if he wanted to dispose of it and he said no. But he was so fascinated with the comment on it because he was at the corner of 10th Street in front of Wanamaker's for years and no one bothered with him. So I was fascinated and he was pleased and he said, "If you like this box, I will really show you a real beautiful one." (He spoke in broken English.) And he said that he left these things, usually, at the bank next door to Wanamaker's, at the entrance. And he said, "You come here Monday, I'll show you the most beautiful shoeshine box in the world."

So I go and I see it. And he's got a throne. He's got a throne with feet. There were five pieces. I never saw anything like it. Now remember that Peggy had that museum. Ernst was a Surrealist. Breton—Surrealist. Duchamp. All of these people were right with us. And it was in the air. And I had just seen the Cornell show. So when I saw that shoeshine box, I knew what it meant. Because it had all the Cubist and the Surrealist. And all unconscious. Because it was Neapolitan. So I thought it was so great that I said to the man, "Would you permit me to take this to the Museum of Modern Art?" He said, "Anything." So I took a truck and took his things and him to the MOMA.

At that time, MOMA had an entrance for painting and sculpture, so I called up Dorothy Miller and it must have been about eleven o'clock by now, and I said, "Dorothy, I have something for the museum," and she said she'd be right down. When we arrived about noon, just by chance, Barr and D'Harnoncourt were going out for lunch. Mr. Barr stopped and said, "Oh, what is this?" Dorothy explained what it was and he turned to Mr. D'Harnoncourt. "I think we should take this for Christmas." Because you see, this was Thanksgiving. "We'll take this for Christmas and give the city a Christmas present. And put it on exhibition in the lobby." He did take it and he did just as he said he would.

It made every newspaper, every magazine. So Nierendorf heard about it, and when I saw him he *looks* at me—he thought he knew me—he says, "Nevelson, what made you go to the museum? Nobody on earth would do that." I said, "Where am I supposed to go with it?"

A little old man. His name was Joe Milone. He used to shoeshine for a living, and this was his dream. This was the kingdom. And he knew that this was beautiful. He knew it. He said that this was the most beautiful shoeshine box in the world. And it was.

*A*t that time I was very aware and I saw and went to everything. Now I never went to Nierendorf without the awareness of why I was going. I knew that I wanted an exhibition of drawings with him, since the Norlyst Gallery was going to show *The Clown Is the Center of the World*. This work I knew was far-out for America at the time. It was very revolutionary—dark old woods with electric eyes, marbles, sand, glass, mirrors on wood for tears, and furniture for the hats. When I went in the room at the gallery, I sat on the east side. He was on the west side facing me. Now I am very conscious about placement, so where I sit, in a room, is important. I always choose to confront a person. I said, "Mr. Nierendorf, I have to have a show with you in April." So he said, "How can I give you a show? I'm all booked up." And he showed me his book. I said, "I'm putting on a very revolutionary show at the Norlyst Gallery and you've *got* to balance it for me with a drawing show." Finally he said, "When is the show?" I said, "April nineteenth." So he said, "All right, you can have a show here April seventh."

But that wasn't all I was there for. I wanted to get a loan. I said, "You know, Mr. Nierendorf, I am renovating my house (I had already found the house on 30th Street) and I find that my expenses are more than I anticipated." And he turns around and says, "Mrs. Prytek, give Mrs. Nevelson a check." Now Mr. Nierendorf was very careful with money, so when he agreed, I nearly fell through the floor.

When he handed me the check he said, "Nevelson, you're going to have every desire in creativity fulfilled." And I was shocked and said, "Mr. Nierendorf, what makes you say that?"

"Well," he said, "I know Picasso and Matisse, I know all the great artists, and I know how they move."

Like Nierendorf, the critics were magnificent. In my life, I must say that I always have been very pleased with critics. From the day I ever showed anything they always gave me praise. They really pointed the way. And so I had certain wonderful things, but the general climate wasn't ready at that time, for my work. I was a soloist.

At the end of the show at the Norlyst, nothing sold. Personally, I didn't think that private people would buy it but I did think that the museums would be ready for that work. But under those circumstances, when the work was returned to me, I had to dismantle the whole show. And for lack of space, I took about two hundred paintings off the stretchers and burnt them in the back lot. I regret it. I believe that what I was doing was right for my awareness at that given time. And in retrospect, even the things that were destroyed, I wish I hadn't. Because they were living reflections of that time.

If there had been *one person* that would have come closer, I think it would have changed a lot of things. Not probably in the ultimate but at the time. Well, I was goddamn angry. That you can be sure. And I'm not talking about sweet little anger, I mean a great ANGER that one contains for years—probably forever to a point. For thirty years I wanted to jump out of every window. I think it's a miracle in retrospect that I didn't lose my mind or ever go into a sanitarium. All my life people have told me not to waste my energies on anger, but I kept anger, I tapped it and tapped it. Anger has given me great strength.

I have a fantasy about Picasso. That every morning, when he got up, they'd delivered to him, hours before, a thousand glasses, and he'd take a wall like that [pointing] and smash them before he'd ever start working.

How hard it was, how long I waited, that was my life, but first I didn't want little small successes. That didn't interest me one bit, it would have embarrassed me. If I didn't sell for thirty years, I just felt that the public wasn't ready. You know, if you have an automobile and it goes a little fast and the others are slow, you're out of key. It is always amazing to me that in the nineteenth century when Cézanne lived, there really wasn't one person on earth who saw eye to eye with him. They may have accepted him and thought him sensitive, but they did not see eye to eye. This should be a lesson to the creative mind and give us courage. Just because there is no one on earth for the moment that sees it, that does not disturb a creative person.

I never for one minute questioned what I had to do. I did not think for one minute that I didn't have what I had. It just didn't dawn on me. And so if you know what you have, then you know that there's nobody on earth that can affect you. But I have an opinion of people in the art world who have these big jobs, who overlook creativity and deprive artists of their rightful place—which is murder. I didn't sell for practically thirty years. That meant I was deprived of a livelihood. Because the people in positions who got salaries were blind, I was deprived. I think there's a great, great injustice. Not just to me, but to all artists. I think it is a great tragedy that right now there may be people that none of us are seeing, because they're not in the stream of this or the stream of that. When a person has a position in a creative way—they have a moral obligation, or they should resign their job. But they don't claim their heritage, so they're unknowing, and anything they don't understand they want to crucify.

There was the anger and the frustration, the whole works, drama, the whole works. I was living a lifetime of things, not one person's. I lived a million lives. And as I say this now and speak about it, I do think that my present work reflects *that* livingness as well as others. It was never lost and still isn't lost, because we just never forget things. It is true we put them in storage, but we don't forget them. All that experience has gone into the work. It still gives me new revelations.

The one thing that must have saved me is, I was a terrific worker and really I thought it was the most important. I must say I don't think it would have been human for anyone on earth to have worked more than I. I had that, you see. I've said that we project, and that you don't really depend so much on people on that level. I wasn't making anything for anybody. I was trying to fulfill a reality for myself. At the time, in the 1940s, I felt that every breath that I took, I was aware, and I didn't feel that there was much breathing outside of myself. And so there I was working and working quite desperately. Now I feel better, thirty years later, only for one reason—that I have made a kind of reality that is a personal reality. Since I did not find a reality, so-called, according to my thinking, on the outside, I have built a whole reality for myself.

I was only on 10th Street for a few months and then my family bought a house for me on East 30th Street. My mother passed away and my father passed away. And I went home. They didn't owe me anything because I hadn't been there for ages, but there were some things left and my brother asked what I would like to have. So I said I want a house in the city. To live in. He said, fine. And I went back, and Ralph Rosenborg lived on the corner of Lexington and 30th Street, and he just walked down the street and found the house for sale. The house was originally owned by a man named Marron, the old man Marron that put in the foundation for Grand Central Station. They were Irish and the whole section of New York around 30th Street they called the Irish Lace Curtain district and Politicians' Row.

I think no more than a week passed after I returned from Maine when Ralph found the house. I wasn't going to wait. And so I bought that house and it wasn't too expensive. An enormous, four-story brownstone house, including a cellar, which made it five stories. And a big backyard where I could work six to eight months a year. A lot of the woods could be stored right in the backyard. It was interesting because at that time houses weren't that available—were not empty, and this one was seventy years old when I bought it. There was a great deal of work that had to be done, and it was done. And Ralph was marvelous. He could do anything. If a ceiling had to be moved two inches or a wall extended or some structural change he would do it in a minute. I had walls taken out and expanded the place.

The house wasn't very wide, but it was long. Any of these brownstones are the same. Each floor was almost like one room and contained a great deal. The ceilings were high, and there were seven marble fireplaces. I had the whole ground floor built like a studio. I bought three sets of furniture, garden furniture, glass tables, and placed them throughout the house, four stories, for myself. So there was a unity throughout the house.

Then the Federation of Modern Painters and Sculptors needed a place to meet, and they knew I had this space, so I gave them the house for meetings.

And then later the Four O'Clock Forums. We had auctions for the Sculptors Guild. That house was really used very well for art. It was almost like a clubhouse in that sense. Only it was a home. And I remember that, on the Four O'Clock Forums, De Kooning was on the panel with others and he spoke so well, and Elaine was taping him and she said to me, "You know that there's so much warmth in here that Bill has never spoken so well." You know, Diana, that's where I had tapestries, Oriental rugs . . . it was modern but also so much of the old combined. Everyone came to the house, Duchamp with his wife, Soulage, Mathieu, various French critics, I can't remember their names. Colette Roberts brought them. All the artists, through one meeting or another, through one forum or another. Lippold came on a panel when he was terribly young and he was just brilliant.

At the time things were interesting. There was Kiesler, all the important galleries having meetings. For instance, there was Julien Levy who used to have soirees where people could speak. It was always pertaining to art. And in a way they made efforts. Now you see, today it's all pretty much business.

During that time we were partying all the time. I knew everyone in the neighborhood, and there was the corner bar. And everyone was drinking and having parties. You were at parties three or four times a week, and good parties in the sense that there was plenty of opening up, liquor and food. I think that the point was the tensions of the outside world and the war and all demanded that people get together somehow.

The house down on 30th Street was interesting, because there was a big backyard. We called the house "The Farm" because the people on the next street, 31st, had a big barn facing like a fence to me, painted red. All you'd have to see were a couple of chickens there. I planted a great many trees, there was a lot of space and yet there were flagstones in the center and we used it about eight months a year. And Teddy Hazeltine, my assistant at that time, would barbecue. He loved to cook and we used to have tables and chairs and eat out all the time. I had no need for going away, because there was so much space.

Teddy came about 1952 and he worked with me. He and I spent a lot of time together, and it was nice. We were working all the time. I was going to say that there was one great fortune in my life. I considered it a great fortune. Some people attract material wealth, some people attract this and that. From the beginning, I somehow attracted people. I never really so-called hired

LN's studio on 30th Street, 1950s. *Jeremiah W. Russell*

people. There would always be somebody that would come into my life and begin working with me. There was always somebody that really helped me in every way. So there must have been some need in me that attracted these people. I think we attract our greatest needs. And that was a great fortune.

It was hard work and lots of work. Great sadness because of the war and the environment and the lack of things.

My last show with Nierendorf was in 1946. In 1948, I had made an appointment with him to discuss my next show. He had gone to Germany on a business trip, returned to New York, and the night before my appointment, a friend called and told me of his death. I always considered Nierendorf my spiritual godfather. He was convinced that I could fulfill myself on a totally creative level, and that meant that he gave me that heritage. I was the only American artist that showed with him on a permanent basis.

After Nierendorf died, I think I didn't show for several years. Mike was in New York sculpting. And I thought that I would lie low. I didn't even try to get a gallery. But I was working all the time, anyway. I worked very hard.

My feeling is that a creative mind has many facets and must have many facets. Now, who is to know when somebody has a breakthrough? Or who is to know who is great? There are some people that maybe we are not recognizing, working quietly somewhere, who don't really want, subconsciously, the responsibility of a public life. I feel if there are artists who have already assumed they are artists, their sensibilities are already ripe and receptive. Take a man like Ryder, whom I have great respect for as a painter in America. He would lock his door and not see people for a long time. Well, his meditation was different. He was aware of this, but he needed this time for something else. Therefore, maybe, he wasn't as keen about other things like so-called success. Because probably he was totally, or almost totally, concentrated in what he had to say. So it is sometimes a bit of a choice in the artist. Then there are artists that may be very shy and really don't choose a public performance till they're ready. So it isn't always that they're not seen; it's that they don't want to be seen.

I used to teach occasionally. One time I taught in Great Neck, and I lived in New York. So I commuted. I had very good students and I wondered: Why? Because I wasn't a teacher in the conventional sense. What I tried to do is shake them up because I wanted them not to sleep through life.

They'd come in and I'd say to each one, "Leave your brain outside, sweetie." I think a mind stands in the way. And I'd sit while they worked. If students are in a studio together they can communicate. There are living things that we're not aware of. One has a spark and puts it down on paper, and something happens in the class. So the environment is important. And the multiplicity of energy and consciousness is important. It's the energy and mentality that's pooled.

One day I said, "I want to ask you—we've been here and working together—and I don't really teach, and yet I am so pleased with the results in this class. Will you tell me what happened?" And they said, "Mrs. Nevelson, you come in and you relieve us of the tensions of everyday living. You have said that if you want to know something, go to another student—don't ask me questions." So I was able to free them. You see, as a child we are taught that children that ask questions are very intelligent. The more questions—why, why, why, why . . . well, what happened is that when I matured I recognized that the people that asked questions were the stupid ones. Because questions are answered within ourselves. Through observation. Not someone telling us. I notice that when I go where there are groups, either parties or lectures or what have you, and there's something I don't understand, I sit back and the thing is *revealed* to me.

So with students, I'd say, "Go to another student." And I'd sit there. Then about the middle of the period, I would look. And then I'd ask one student that I knew and who was working on something you could cut with a knife, something terra cotta, "Do you mind if I give a demonstration on your piece?" And while all these students were around I'd take a knife and cut and give them planes and show them that this plane and that was like building an architectural building. I used to get so exhausted from the class that I was glad there was a bar next door to the train station. I'd go right in there and relax myself before I'd take the train home.

I taught that time about four years. When I thought I was getting a little stale, I'd leave. Four years was my limit and then it became sort of routine.

I was on a very good panel once at Mount Holyoke in the late fifties. The college was having an exhibition of Kline, De Kooning, myself, and others. So one of the panel members felt that the work of the Abstract Expressionists wasn't valid, and that the artists that signed them were just egocentrics and wanted their names big, splashed over it. I felt it would be unfair to let these students go away with the thought that someone with authority could dismiss a whole school of painting. So I counteracted what she said and told the students that I thought it was the most important movement in America. That those signatures were a part of the painting and were totally valid. If I were to teach young children in the beginning the first lesson would be for that child to write his or her name a thousand times a day on the blackboard. So that each child's signature would identify that child. And each child would have a sense of self. Now I'm not talking about ego, that's on the surface. But the sense of self is one's center. So there's a cliché: Oh, the sun doesn't revolve around you. Well, the sun *does* revolve around each individual and, really, our lives are our universes. So I think it is very important for the person that is doing a work of art to identify with self.

A man stood up in an audience once when Artists Equity was having a panel in New York several years ago and asked me, "Why do we have to sign our work? Why do we need signatures?" And I said, "Look, if you or I sign a check for a million dollars and go to the bank, no one is going to honor it. But if Rockefeller signs a check for a million dollars, he can get that million dollars. That is the need for a signature."

My sister Anita and I went to Mexico twice in one year, 1951. We wanted to see particularly the art. I'll tell you why I wanted to go. I knew what Mexican art was and I had seen pictures and I had already worked with Diego Rivera, and I also wanted to go to Costa Rica to see the archaeological sites there. And of course when we got to Mexico City you had to engage a private plane, and there were no commercial planes. We never quite made it to Costa Rica. But what I found in Mexico City itself was just overwhelming.

I visited Diego and Frieda there, too. They had built an adobe house with cactus all around it in Mexico City—I think they had had that house already when they were in New York in the thirties. Diego was doing a mural in Mexico, but he was already ill. He had cancer. And Frieda was in the hospital and he asked me to go and see her, so I did. She was marvelous. I think she knew she was passing away, but it appeared that didn't bother her. She was just as sweet and cheerful as she could be, laughing and carrying on. And soon after that, she passed away. Diego went on and then I think he went to Russia. Anyway, that was the last time I saw him.

Then we went from Mexico City to Yucatan . . . but before we came back to Mexico City, I went first to Oaxaca. Yucatan was a world of forms that at once I felt was mine, a world where East and West met, a world of geometry and magic. Of course the pyramids. I think they're so superior to the

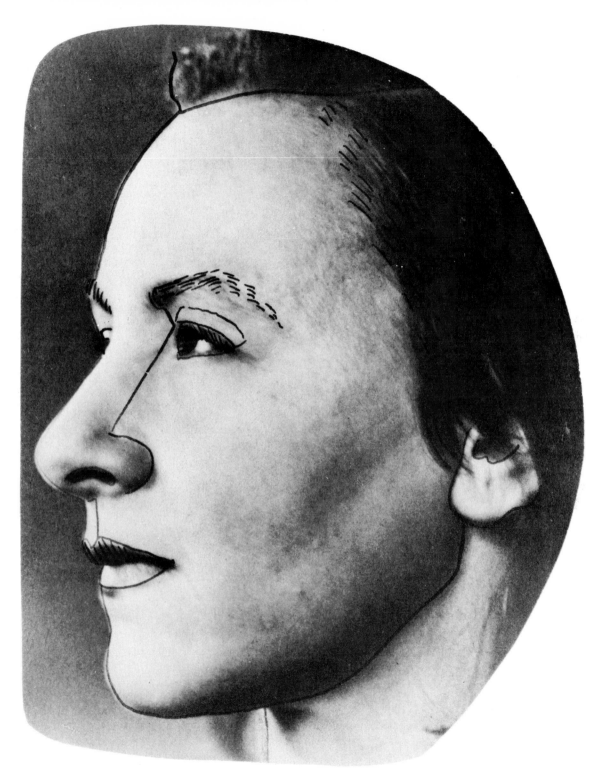

Lotti Jacobi photograph of LN, which LN drew on

Majesty, etching, 18″ x 21⅝″, by LN, no date. *Whitney Museum of American Art*

Egyptians'. The sculpture, the power, and the organization was overwhelming. And the climate. What is interesting is that those two centers, Egypt and Mexico, are warm climates. When you walk up the pyramids, you go into the ethers. You get the refined air and you get light-headed. I walked up, but not too far.

Just the visual, to look at the strength of it, the balance of it, the rightness of it, makes you feel that . . . in the past they would talk about primitive countries. But when you see their sundials and the way everything was done, truly, *we* are the primitive country. And we are. Because when you go to any of those sacred places, say to Yucatan, and see the sacred land that they had for their priests, it was roped off. They used to measure off the land that was sacred. Now, there was nothing around that area that would intrude on those priests' minds. And no one else was permitted to go on this sacred land. A larger spiritual experience would be possible then, in that arrangement. A planned arrangement.

Well, when I came back to New York and passed St. Patrick's Cathedral and then looked in Saks Fifth Avenue's windows, I thought how barbaric we are. Say you go into a church and then you walk out and instead of meditating, you're already caught in looking at material things in the windows. You're distracted instantly from any kind of spiritual communication. And so I reversed totally for myself and felt that *we* are the primitive ones. They were the highly organized ones. They were the sophisticates. According to my book, Mexico and its sculpture and pyramids is number one. It will stand up to anything on this earth.

I really started to have one-woman exhibitions again in New York when I decided to show with Colette Roberts in the Grand Central Moderns. I showed before that but in group shows. I showed anywhere I was asked and I don't even want to mention names of the places I've showed. That's what I mean when I say I'm a yes woman. If they asked me, I showed. I didn't care where. I know sculptors that won't show in certain galleries, they say the light isn't good. I don't care anything about that. What I'm interested in in my own life is to do the work. I remember a critic asked me, "How the hell did you dare to show at so and such a place?" And I said, "They asked me." It was just as direct as that. My feeling is, show wherever you can. I've always said it to everyone.

Circus Wagon, etching, 17⅝″ x 14⅞″, by LN, no date. *Whitney Museum of American Art*

I showed the first etchings at Lotte Jacobi's gallery in 1950 that I did on copper and zinc plates, Diana. Done at Atelier 17. Grippi had said, "You must come in because I need some professionals." And I said, "Grippi, I can't stand those tools, and I don't want to learn that thing. I'm not a dentist." He said, "You come and I will show you things where you don't need to use these tools." So I said, "All right, I'll come." And lightning struck me twice. He gave me two things that were the key to what I needed. One was a can opener, and the other was material, all kinds of material, lace particularly. And the first thing I did, I put it in acid and where I scratched the acid ate into it and gave me what I loved. It corroded. And so I thought, "Oh, this is marvelous, it's quick and direct." And so I stayed on. In one month I made thirty etchings, and I gave the plates to the Museum of Modern Art in the 1960s. I did them almost blindfolded. And the feel of it, I loved it. I really loved them, because it gave me so much freedom to create, instead of technique.

Also I showed at the Stable, in 1954, but just one piece. I was invited. And I know the piece I showed. It was terra cotta, a moving one. One of the ones I gave in a group to the Whitney in the 1960s.

Through personal choice and necessity, I never became involved with a group of artists. I don't belong to any movement. Of course, there is no mistake that the times I was living in had influence on me. We pool our energies with other creative people. I feel that, say, if some of our people weren't around where sparks fly, maybe I would not have come to this. That *must* be. My work is bound to be related to that of others. I think what we do is take what *we* understand of both ourselves and what we see around us. Our own nature makes a selection; it selects which things please you more. When you feel that rapport, you work along those lines, consciously or not. I don't mean you copy. But I think when you live in a hunk of time, you reflect a hunk of time. What takes place in it.

But you know . . . I wouldn't feel in the right place if I was in the stream of Abstract Expressionism. Now I think they are marvelous. I love their art, and I love their energy. Nevertheless I had to go my own way. Yes, I believe artists reflect their time, but they have to stand on their own two feet . . . not on someone else's. I chose at quite an early age to be a soloist. Because I realized that the rhythms of people are different. Consequently, I wouldn't assume to impose that on somebody else. And by the same token, I had to make my decisions, I had to make my moves. Everything came back to *me*.

Installation of *Moving-Static-Moving Figures*, terra cotta, by LN, ca. 1945.
Whitney Museum of American Art

Night Presence IV, Cor-ten steel, 22″ high, by LN, 1972, Park Avenue, New York City.
Diana MacKown

And even now, when I think of a school of, say—Conceptual Art, or Abstract Art . . . I recognize it but I felt I wanted to move on my own lines.

I'm a totally unorthodox artist, but that does not annihilate any movement. Now I would like, and I've done it before, to establish that I think the Abstract Expressionist painters in America were vital, subjective. I think it was the most important direction. Consequently, I'm going to say right now, which I've said before, that artists will have to come back to that to finish the job. Here's the thing. People take too many licenses. I'd like to compare it with music, to composing. Now, when people hear music, they study and go to all sorts of concerts, et cetera, all their lives, to appreciate and be moved by these composers. And it's a life study, just to get a finer tone, to identify with a finer tone. But in art, the eye, no one has said that the public has to become educated. So people just take it for granted. They go in and they say, "I like this. I don't like it." "Why do you like it?" "Well, I like it better, for no reason, and who cares?" That to me is absolutely such stupidity. You can't look at the Abstract Expressionists in that sense. If you really want to get a deeper feeling, it means that you really have to be with it. It isn't that easy. But the general public did not give it the same attention that they would have to music, and they were lost. Because they weren't seeing objects that they were used to. So you see when now the artist turned to so-called Realism, everybody that couldn't move and walk along and take the time to learn about that search was so happy because they began to see objects, again, that they could identify with.

I think all great innovations are built on rejections. In our time, in the work we break formal form. It has been attempted for many years now; form has broken. But then another form has come out of that broken form. It is not formless. And even formless has a form.

It was really the climate of New York City that made Abstract Expressionism possible. Do you notice, Diana, more and more I have a feeling of New York City as if it were a person? Well, like it was a person, you could say that it's an innovator. Because what we are seeing throughout the world, big buildings and skyscrapers are really a takeoff on New York City. It's the model of every other twentieth-century city.

When I look at the city from my point of view, I see New York City as a *great big sculpture.* I saw the Empire State Building when it was going up. So many buildings that have gone up and come down. And the skyline is in constant change, through light and through its great activity. But it's only later, when we first get to the Lever Building and the Seagram Building, to the structural steel and glass skyscrapers, that the architecture of the individual building really interested me. These buildings became weightless and airy through its structure and transparency, through the use of glass. They're not pulled down by gravity to solid rock. The ground floor level of the Lever Brothers Building is lifted up so it floats and opens and lets in light, and the Seagram Building is set back from Park Avenue. And so you have that great luxury of space in front of it.

The World Trade Center is two giant cubes and the tallest cubes in the city. They stand there among the rest of the sculpture-city and they are fine. They're magnificent. When the lights go on at night they're touching beyond the heavens. But when you think of the concept of building involved in the World Trade Center, it has set a precedent and challenge to the world that the human mind has encompassed the engineering of that space. From that point of view the World Trade Center is a landmark. And you can understand, if you want to tie it up with the evolution of humanity, how the human mind is going to have to move and expand to accept it.

Of course the Abstract Expressionists started in New York. So you can see where we identify somewhere or it's in the air. It's in the air and you take it. Seeing those high risers, bigger and bigger and bigger . . . you couldn't think of little paintings or little pieces. And I also never wanted to make a piece that they put on a table for decoration. That didn't interest me a bit. No parlor pieces. I didn't want that. *This* is what I have lived in. When you think that my whole adult life almost, summer and winter, I was here . . . the only thing I can say, thinking of these great buildings and the scale of everything and my own energy, it was just a natural. Now if you take a car and you go up on the East River and come down the West Side Highway toward evening or toward morning, when the buildings are silhouetted and they are not disturbed by that much activity, you will see that many of my works are real reflections of the city. I visited Georgia O'Keeffe . . . the mountains are *her* landscape. Well, New York City is mine.

Now, New York City was the art center. I knew De Kooning, Pollock, Kline, all of them. I have had a lot of artists around me. And I adore them. That's not the point. But I've never really lived among them. I never went, for instance, to a summer colony where there were artists. I may have gone for a

Moon Spikes IV, wood painted black, 36½″ x 42″, by LN, 1955. *Jeremiah W. Russell*

Skowhegan School of Painting and Sculpture: LN (left), Willard Cummings, Bernard Langlais, and Bette Davis, 1970s. *Diana MacKown*

day. Or two. But I didn't affiliate. I was pretty much of a soloist. Had I joined

something—a movement—and decided to leave, that would have been fair. But then people are so strange, they would have felt and still do feel that you're a traitor to their cause. Well, an artist who has two feet and can stand on them doesn't feel that he wants anyone to trample on him. I'm an outsider because I wouldn't permit anyone to bother me. That's the price you pay for freedom.

I've lived alone for years, and I slowly cut out social life. I leave the world to the world. I just do my work. Which is a great marvelous thing. I certainly wouldn't want to be on earth if I didn't have that facing me. You see, Diana, I was a little different than others. I was busy. I'm a work horse. I like to work. I always did. I think that there is such a thing as energy, creation overflowing. And I always felt that I have this great energy and it was bound to sort of burst at the seams, so that my work automatically took its place with a mind like mine. I've never had a day when I didn't want to work. I've never had a day like that. And I knew that a day I took away from the work did not make me too happy. I just feel that I'm in tune with the right vibrations in the universe when I'm in the process of working. I always felt right when I was right here. And even if I didn't want to compose, so I painted or stacked the pieces or something. In my studio I'm as happy as a cow in her stall. That's the only place where everything is all right.

The tools are put away at night and the studio is swept down and the things which you will want for tomorrow morning are placed out. So when you go to the studio, it's like kneading bread, or doing anything: you start working. Everything is clean, is nice. You are very happy. You start working. Well . . . actually we don't really work, but unfortunately we don't have words to express what we're doing. I don't like the word *work* because it isn't, but I haven't found another word to define what I do. I've thought of it for a long time. I think *work* is a bad word, because *work* means labor and this is not labor.

Creation itself is a dimension, you see. Creation itself. The word *creation* is like the earth, the volcanoes, the mother who has her labor pains, and this rain, whatever, all the emotions in the ocean, the turmoil. Creation is there. It isn't where the water's clear. Creation means you are in the labor pains of something, in the great activity. I think creation is living. Now one breathes day and night. And if you don't breathe, you're not going to live, so you have

29 Spring Street.
Diana MacKown

to breathe. Breath and life are together. Well, when I'm working it's like breathing. I don't have to say, oh, this is going to be this and this is . . . and if I don't work, I'm not breathing. I have to breathe to live.

I trained myself not to make mistakes, because look—you make a mistake, it isn't that you go back, but your whole time clock changes and your attitude and all. I don't like too many errors. They color your brain. I think some people live a whole life of errors. But I don't demand perfection. I never want perfection—I hate the word. I think that it's *arrogant*. And the word *masterpiece* offends me no end. I feel that words can be deadly because if you get caught in them they can kill you. I've seen this happen. When I taught, for instance, people would say, oh, I want to make a masterpiece, oh, I want perfection. Oh . . . well, they never got anywhere. When you put this thing in front of you, this nonexistent, the closer you get the more it moves, then they get discouraged and they never get beyond that. I remember in art class, a few people . . . one was a woman sculptor and she could never finish a piece. She would get just so far and she had a block. And there was another man, who used to draw and draw and draw and he threw them all away. They should have kept moving and not permitted these blocks. That's why the word *perfection* is dangerous, because it can defeat people, artists included. And anyway, there is no such thing. Who are we humans to think we know what perfection is, or masterpieces? You don't ask . . . when you breathe. Well, I live every day like you're breathing. That's creation, that's living, and that's art. Because the areas that I can see consciousness moving, doesn't mean striving for perfection. Maybe we're in a place that surpasses it. Like clouds above clouds.

I'm very fast. Not in everything. But in art. I suppose you might say I'm not frightened. I'll try anything and I do, and usually I bring it to a conclusion for my own mind. I work at a certain speed and I like it, because it means you're not taking as much time to meditate. I like excitement. I don't like a meditative life. From the beginning I liked the thought that you didn't have to sleep over a thing . . . that you're active. I believe that activity is intelligence. You see, if you bring in the conscious mind—oh, this is right or this is wrong—it won't be spontaneous. I hate the word *intellect* or the word *logic*—logic is against nature. And *analysis,* another vulgar word. If you're tied up seriously with something, you don't have to analyze every minute. When you breathe, you don't think every minute, I'm breathing. But if you are going fast, you're not letting the conscious mind do so much thinking. It's there, but you are not letting it take over. You're permitting the whole consciousness and unconsciousness and all things to work with you. So you're tapping everything, like a gold mine. Going through it and tapping every bit of it in a second. So I use speed; I like it. And I really think that every great artist is wound up on this rhythm. Is wound up on this great energy that takes you into new areas. Because the speed makes it more vital and gives you the intensity of greater reality.

When I was in my youth, in the twenties and thirties, I was a marvelous draftsman. When I used a line, it was like a violin. I could use it light and I could use it heavy, and I used it that way, then I was free. I might have been bottled up in other things, but I was free to let my hand go. Because as I told you, I love movement. So I didn't stop with it. I didn't have to measure. You know I have never taken a yardstick to measure anything in my work. Never. It would offend me to think I would have to measure something, because I *feel* it. And not only that, I am aware of the human mind. Not only the visual mind but the living mind. Now think if I stopped this mind and took a yardstick and stopped to measure. Think of what would happen to that piece . . . if I had to take and measure . . . the minute I would stop it I would feel that I committed death toward it. It stops the whole flow, it stops the bloodstream, it stops the body from where it was. It arrests it. I'd rather let it move and move and then let it stay. That means that the creativity was not stopped. The flow of thinking and the awareness wasn't stopped.

I remember once in the early thirties I was invited to a celebrated American sculptor's studio in New York. He had a studio near 14th Street, and as I walked in, he had an armature for a horse. (He had commissions for public parks and all.) It was enormous and made of wood put together and I was overwhelmed with its grandeur. Then the sculptor had about a thousand photographs of the piece of work in progress—it was a horse with a person on it and when I saw all the photographs and how he had overworked, the end result—the finished piece—was dead. And I clocked it. My God—the armature was *it;* the sculpture was static!

In that place of awareness I will say, like a great singer or musician would say they have perfect pitch . . . in that way I have a taste of freedom to let my eye do the judging. Now some people use words like *intuition*, which I dislike. That is a label, intuition. It's because they don't know what to say. And it's very deceptive. People think all they have to do is sit down and they're going to sit on intuition [laughs]. Well, you can throw garbage into intuition, you know. So I don't particularly like that word, as much as people think. Of course I tap things . . . but we can call it maybe another name.

I go to the sculpture, and my eye tells me what is right for me. When I compose, I don't have anything but the material, myself, and an assistant. I compose right there while the assistant hammers. Sometimes it's the material that takes over; sometimes it's me that takes over. I permit them to play, like a seesaw. I use action and counteraction, like in music, all the time. Action and counteraction. It was always a relationship—my speaking to the wood and the wood speaking back to me. That is probably why I did go into assemblage and then ensemblage: I permit the medium to speak to me, too. I'm always there to guide it, but I don't superimpose, say, like a blueprint and it has to be precision and all. I hate that, because that to me is what you call dictating. I permit it to move to how I feel, how it weighs and how it moves. In other words, my feeling and the sculpture become one. It's a love affair, and it becomes one.

I love the immediacy. When I look at it, does it look right to me, does it weigh right to me, does it act right to me? I'm sure of certain things. If my eye and my feeling of that space don't meet, I won't use it. I try playing with light and shade, the different sizes and mediums and weights. And I work till I think it's right for me. It's addition and subtraction. You add or subtract until you feel . . . the form, the principle, that something that makes the house stand; that makes you stand.

You see, I think that we have measurements in our bodies. Measurements in our eyes. Look, dear, we walk on two feet. So we're vertical. That doesn't mean the work has to be vertical, but it means that there is a weight within ourselves, or this flight. All these things are within the being: weight and measure and color. And if the work is good work, it is built on these laws and principles that we have within ourselves. So when you use a vertical line or a horizontal line, or a texture or the way the shadow falls on a thinner piece or a heavier piece, it all kind of satisfies something in the soul—or, I don't like the word *soul*, satisfies something within the deed. And you know it's right for you, and you're satisfied.

I don't say I'm born with a perfect eye, but I'm born with the rightness of my being. I have a mind for what I need. That's why I can do so much. I just don't have any trouble. I feel maybe someone will say, "How sure she is of herself." So I restrain myself from saying it. But I am sure. Let's face it. You see, they said at four years old already I was creative. And so I use that and I understand it—maybe like Mozart knew his music. You are or you are not.

Well, I knew I had it, and I also knew I had the energy of many people. I've always had it. So I'm prolific, to begin with; but I'm also prolific because I know how to use time. I prepare my materials for the next day. I get up, six in the morning. And I wear cotton clothes so that I can sleep in them or I can work in them—I don't want to waste time. I go to the studio, and usually I put in pretty much of a big day. And very often, almost all the time (I think I have a strong body), it wears me out. The physical body is worn out before the creative. When I finish, I come in and go to sleep if I'm tired, have something to eat. Time as such doesn't involve me. I think here I could really use time, feeling that a minute could be eternity, eternity could be a minute. So that is measured by man, not by creation. I think humans have measured things to the majority, but the person that is being on another level can't take the clock with him.

Sometimes I could work two, three days and not sleep and I didn't pay any attention to food, because . . . a can of sardines and a cup of tea and a piece of stale bread seemed awfully good to me. You know, I don't care about food and my diet has very little variety. I read once that in her old age Isak Dinesen only ate oysters and drank champagne, and I thought what an intelligent solution to ridding oneself of meaningless decision-making.

I gauge my dentist appointments or if I want to check up with a doctor or anything like that for a certain period of the year so as not to superimpose on me. That gives me a little rest period too. I spend a lot of time in the house, and I have folding tables. I may want to work here, or I may want to work in another studio. So nothing is too static. I don't like a chair that doesn't have a back. And I don't want anyone to come and park themselves. I have a way of living that suits me and I'm not pushing to make others comfortable. I want to make myself more comfortable, not only physically but in every state.

So you see, the economy of time is not only in the studio, but it is economy of all kinds of time. And if you regulate and understand it, can you imagine how the human mind clocks in? There's no waste of consciousness. So that is why and how I produce a lot, because I understand these things. And also how to use my mind, in the sense that I don't clutter it with things that don't pertain to the very *act* of doing it. I believe that we can clean our minds out and not carry too much waste. Anything that's cluttered is a constipation of some sort. Anything—a house, a closet. If it's clear you can put something in it, but if it's crowded you can't put anything in it. So I always started with that kind of premise.

I take my mind out and put it on the table. I take silver polish or whatever and rags and sponges and clean it up and clear it up and keep it shiny. Look, if you get a little splinter in a finger, it can infest your whole hand and you get sick. I won't permit a thought to enter into my consciousness if I don't feel it's a healthy thought, and the good healthy thoughts I have for myself, for me. I feel that in my own life, I have made my own reality. I'm not seeking the concept truth. It does not interest me because I don't want to know everything, and I don't want to clutter myself. So I have *broken* the concept of a rigid truth or a yardstick. I have been able to make myself more comfortable by reorienting a thought or whatever to suit my kind of thinking. A truth isn't a truth to me, a lie isn't a lie. If I were to accept academically these words and what they stand for, it would kill me immediately. If a so-called lie will be a tool for me to fulfill myself, I'll use it and have no morals about it. And if a so-called truth can destroy me, the hell with it. I cling to my own standards as much as I can. I don't give a damn. If it is more comfortable for me, that's fine. That's my truth.

Maybe because so little of the other things on earth interest me, my total being is pretty much right in the work. I don't go to concerts or shows because I'm so tired of directors and man-made things. I've never gone in for many movies and still don't. You know, you have to go. And you have to sit with a lot of people and you see something that was manufactured. Even at that given time when it was an innovation, when I was young, I must say that I didn't move into those areas very much. Because my own life was very active. Very dramatic. It took all my emotions to survive and I couldn't go into a movie and lose myself even in Charlie Chaplin, or even in Buster Keaton. I just couldn't. The only one that *really* I felt great about was Greta Garbo. That's very interesting, but it's true. But I think that my work takes me to another place, and so I don't quite like sitting around. I'd rather be in the studio where the next thing is a new creation and wasn't planned.

Another thing about creation is that every day it is like it gave birth, and it's always kind of an innocent and refreshing. So it's always virginal to me, and it's always a surprise. I feel in principle or in the deep relationship of the vision and the object and the subject that there is a *unity* and that is *fresh* constantly. You make a living thing through your livingness. You move, you live, you breathe, so it enters . . . enters . . . enters. Each piece seems to have a life of its own. Every little piece or every big piece that I make becomes a very living thing to me, very living. I could make a million pieces; the next piece gives me a whole new thing. It is a new center. Life in total at that particular time. And that's why it's right. That reaffirms my life.

There isn't a thing I want to keep. I don't believe in keeping anything. Some artists don't want to give up a painting or a work, but I'm very fluid that way. I love to see my work move and be placed. I don't need it around me because I don't want my mind to be cluttered. I want my mind to be open and clear to do the next work. The excitement of my life is when I'm working and making decisions: when I put things together and *how* I put them together. I call that the livingness or the essence of aliveness. Because you are totally alive when you are doing it. You're tapping the real fibers of what life is all about.

*N*ow in the reality that I built for myself, what did I do? I took one tone. I gave the work order; I neutralized it by one tone. One of the reasons I originally started with black was to see the forms more clearly. Black seemed the strongest and clearest. But then somehow as I worked and worked and worked . . . it pleased me. You see, one thing about my way of thinking—I didn't want it to be sculpture and I didn't want it to be painting. I didn't want to make something. I think it's stupid to want to make anything. Why make anything? You know, there's an awful lot of crap on this earth and we don't want to fill it with any more. Let the air breathe. But—the thing is that it's something *beyond* that we make. My work has never been black to me to begin with. I never think of it that way. I don't make sculpture and it isn't black and it isn't wood or anything, because I wanted something else. I wanted an essence.

Now ordinarily, you know, people think wood is wood and black wood is black wood. Once when I was speaking to students at Queens College—I never was what you call a lecturer—this student has a pencil and she says, "I

LN, 1956. *Jeremiah W. Russell*

was invited to take notes for the paper, and of course your work is black and it is wood and it is sculpture." So I said, "Well now, if that's what you're sitting here for and that's what it appears like to you then you've missed the whole thing." Because I really don't deal in that. It's like—there's an opera, this great singer, and you're listening to the sound. Well, if you're a teacher or a musician you might get caught in the technique—but the audience is not supposed to do that. Their spirit is supposed to be soaring into this grandeur of harmony. And some of these opera stars probably studied twenty, thirty years just to give this great performance. So I told them, I said, "If this doesn't touch you, your nervous system or something, so that you can sit there cold-blooded and call it wood, and call it black and say it's sculpture, then I've missed the boat, because for definition, these are three-dimensional, but what it should do is bring you into the fourth."

Later I said, "Now I've made my point. Of course the material is wood. Of course it's black, and of course it's sculpture. But those are the mechanics!" When you look at a Rolls-Royce, a Silver Cloud, you don't say, "Oh, they've got guts to make 'em run." Unless you're a mechanic or something. You just look at it and say, "Isn't the Silver Cloud great?" and then get in it (I was in it once) and you won't believe it. Maybe you've been in it. It took me all these years, but I was in it, I'll say, once. I couldn't believe the difference. It was heaven, a silver cloud. Well, that's the difference I feel in work. It's got to be silver cloud; not caught in the matter of three dimensions.

So the work that I do is not the matter and it isn't the color. I don't use color, form, wood as such. It adds up to the in-between place, between the material I use and the manifestation afterwards; the dawns and the dusks, the places between the land and the sea. The place of in-between means that all of this that I use—and you can put a label on it like "black"—is something I'm using to say something else.

About what black . . . the illusion of black means to me: I don't think I chose it for black. I think it chose *me* for saying something. You see, it says more for me than anything else. In the academic world, they used to say black and white were no colors, but I'm twisting that to tell you that for me it is the total color. It means totality. It means: contains all. You know, this is one of the most interesting things to me, that people have identified with black all their lives and, for some reason, they identify black with death or finish. Well, it may be that in the third dimension black is considered so. It's a myth, really. But after painting, using color . . . Now, I don't see colors, as I've often said, the way others do. I think color is magnificent. It's an illusion. It's a mirage. It's a rainbow. But why not? It's great. I was considered quite a colorist, and I can appreciate that artists in the past centuries used color—that it was right. And they were symphonies. Certainly I'm a great admirer of Bonnard or Matisse. I think Bonnard used color of that tone, we'll call it not a minor key but a major key—the treble clef. Well, he reached a symphony of color. Now if you can do that and you *want* that it almost becomes no color, because it's a mirage of light. There isn't a color that isn't of that intensity if you can get that essence and *not* think of it as color. Not only black and white and gold and silver, but you can also go to the rainbow and you can see in the sky the purples and the blues.

But when I fell in love with black, it contained all color. It wasn't a negation of color. It was an acceptance. Because black encompasses all colors. Black is the most aristocratic color of all. The only aristocratic color. For me this is the ultimate. You can be quiet and it contains the whole thing. There is no color that will give you the feeling of totality. Of peace. Of greatness. Of quietness. Of excitement. I have *seen things* that were transformed into black, that took on just greatness. I don't want to use a lesser word. Now, if it does that for things I've handled, that means that the *essence* of it is just what you call—alchemy.

Now in convention, alchemy means *transformation* of something into gold. Well I think that's *exactly* what I've done with it. Now if one wants to read what I'm saying and say, oh, well, she didn't get it right, I don't care. What I want to say is that *that* is *true* for the way I understand it.

Of course, what's interesting is, some of our artists, the contemporary artists in America—as of now a couple have passed away—they came to black, and when you spoke to them . . . it was not that they looked at black and said, *ohhhh*. They came to it through a long process. Now when Ad Reinhardt used black, he used black from a totally different point of view. He had a lot of philosophical things. He went through the mind till he came to a quiet statement. See, I'm making a distinction between Reinhardt and myself. He came to it philosophically. I came to it . . . maybe subconsciously there's something going on. Maybe this is the distinction. I just feel looking—the eye—I just feel *looking* at it is the most satisfying of all things. You see, gold metal is very beautiful. But it shines and it *blinds* you. When you use black it doesn't *hit* you. I just think I'm blessed to see the great harmony. I see great music that's harmony. I think it's a totality. Not a depth, but a total song that is constantly singing to greatness. Emotionally, it may have great sorrow, or great joy . . . but it seems to me that it's an essence. That's why I use the word *alchemy*. What do I care if it's considered used with gold? I consider that since *we* are speaking a language to *express* something, I don't care what we use. If you want to use a rag instead of a royal velvet, but the rag will do the thing, who cares?

We will continue on black because I think if I speak about it every day for the rest of my life, I wouldn't finish about what it really means. Another thing. When you think that . . . say, at night you see black, and yet put on the light and you see the colors. First you need to press the button. You want a great deal of light in here, and you can press that little button of electricity, and you get light. But it's altogether sort of a mirage. It's altogether kind of an illusion. Humans don't quite want to accept that. You see, the human mind must have some rest, so it's given itself certain laws. It says: this is stable, this is static. We say: this is red. But it's all a rainbow and a mirage. When darkness comes, you don't see any of that, and light's constantly changing. In the evening, a certain tone; then an hour later . . . and it's a constant new. But what we do is we *arrest* it. We see something and we want that fleeting thing for eternity, and we are the ones that arrest it. In memory you had a moment of joy, and you say, "I want to remember this forever." And you arrest it and it's your tool forever.

You see . . . and then the shadow. The shadow, you know, is as important as the object. Now I have taken titles for myself, since I live with myself, most of myself, all my life. I gave myself the title "The Architect of Shadow." Why? You see, shadow and everything else on earth actually is moving. Movement— that's in color, that's in form, that's in almost everything. Shadow is fleeting . . . and I arrest it and I give it a solid substance. I think I gave it as strong a form as the material object that gives me the shadow . . . probably stronger. More valid. And that satisfies me . . . that a shadow can have the weight and form of other things. I arrest it and I give it architecture as solid as anything can be.

I made a black wedding cake . . . this was on 30th Street. You know that great big piece that's in the Brooklyn Museum? That's one of the first major pieces, it's called *First Personage*—1956. What happened was, I acquired those planks and things, and I got so involved in my work that I really was creating a novel, because I had myself being the bride . . . it was my autobiography in that sense. So I did then *First Personage*, and that must be at least six and a half feet tall and it's two inches wide—thick. In width it's about two and one-half feet but I mean in depth it's only about two inches. The interesting thing, while I was filing and working away at it there was a knot where the mouth was supposed to be, just a plain knot, and I, being so concentrated, all of a sudden I saw this knot, mouth moving. And the whole thing was black by then and it frightened me. At that time I was so geared in that I . . . made . . . a black wedding cake. I'm always taking these trips, you see, and I suppose this trip I didn't have a bridegroom, but I had a wedding cake. If you're going without a bridegroom, naturally it's going to be a black wedding cake. Then I made a bridge to cross over. The bridge was a single two-inch lath, but it was about six or seven feet long and I put a few little so-called houses . . . a couple of little wood blocks on either end. To change the texture of light I glued a one-half-inch-wide ribbon of black velvet to one edge of the lath. See, I'm returning to that period. There's a certain virility there and simplicity, you know. Anyway . . . I crossed that bridge. I was caught in that state of mind and then I was coming out of it. I realized you couldn't go on that bridge, that it was impossible for a human to go on that bridge and that there are no black wedding cakes and that personage was sculpture. But they had all become realities. And so I had to fight to come back.

So I don't think it's difficult to see where people move into different areas, and some go out of their bodies and never know how to return. If you study metaphysics you'll see that we can get out of ourselves. And maybe there is a bit of danger—so what? You have to have the courage to try it. What would you do with your life if you didn't risk it?

I had been through it, and I didn't want those pieces around me, so I gave them all away as fast as I could. I couldn't have lived with them being in the house. Now, of course, I'm divorced from them.

The first stacked wall I did in the house on 30th Street. That big black wall that is in the Museum of Modern Art (*Sky Cathedral*). That went to the MOMA in 1956, so I must have done it in 1954–1955, but I changed it. I redesigned it for the space up in the museum.

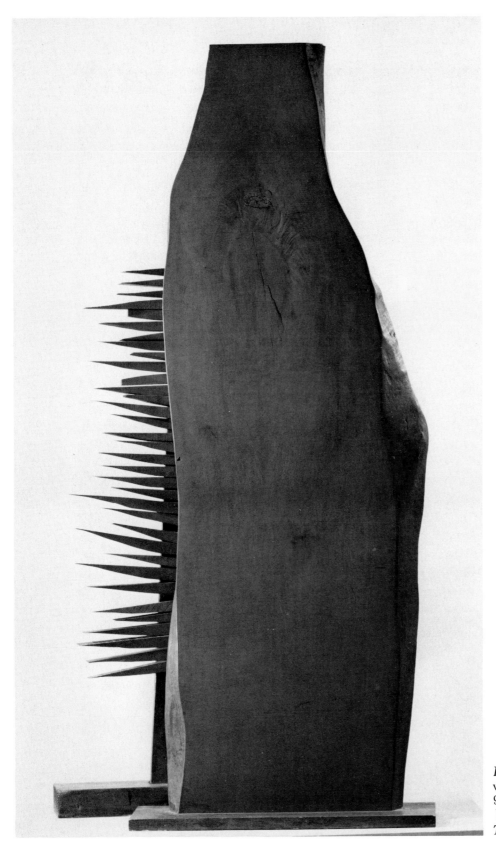

First Personage,
wood painted black,
94″ high (maximum),
by LN, 1956.
The Brooklyn Museum

That was when Marcel Duchamp came down to the house, just a few months before that wall went to the MOMA. So it was in the house yet. I had met a painter who was sort of a liaison between French people and Americans. So she called me about a French critic and his wife and Duchamp and his wife that would like to come and see me. She wanted to bring them to my house.

Well, when we all sat down, it didn't take Duchamp long to speak French, like he couldn't speak English. Maybe he couldn't speak as good an English as he did later. He implied and he thought, in translating, that I asked him his opinion on my work. Because none of the big black walls were seen yet. And I turned around and said, "You just tell Mr. Duchamp that I did not ask for his opinion." And his wife, Teeny, said, "Oh, I think he misunderstands!" And I said fine and we became the best of friends. When I moved down here to Spring Street they came down here and were darling. And they invited me over. When I went to his home for dinner, he had a chair like a king, high-backed and all. I heard later that Max Ernst gave it to him. Their apartment was very, very lovely because Teeny has a great elegance and he had a great elegance.

I attribute the walls to this. I had loads of energy. I mean, energy and energy and loads of creative energy. And no matter how much space—now it's different, but at that time if I'd had a city block it wouldn't have been enough, because I had this energy that was flowing like an ocean into creativity. Now I think a brook is beautiful, and a lake you can look at and it's just peaceful and glorious, but I identify with the ocean. So I did begin to stack them. It was a natural. It was a flowing of energy.

I think there is something in the consciousness of the creative person that adds up, and the multiple image that I give, say, in an enormous wall gives me so much satisfaction. There is great satisfaction in seeing a splendid, big, enormous work of art. I'm fully aware that the small object can be very precious and very important. But to me personally, I think there is something in size and scale. We have all heard of quantity, of quality. I want a lot of quality in a lot of quantity.

When I first claimed the word *environment* for myself I was in Japan. I was on a panel and I said, "I am the grandmother of environment." Nobody did until I did—make a whole environment. It was *Moon Garden + One*, 1958, at the Grand Central Moderns. When I showed before with Colette [Roberts] they had a gallery on East 56th Street. Then they moved to 1080

Madison Avenue, and that's where I had *Ancient Games and Ancient Places*

and later, *Moon Garden + One.* My shows always had themes.

Ancient Games and Ancient Places was environment but, again, no one was ready for it. Let me explain. Since art, particularly sculpture, is so living, so very living, naturally you want all of life, so you make a total environment. In one way it is a disservice to discuss separate works because it's the total environment that is important. It's not only sculpture, it is a whole world. All my shows have had a title of one piece. *Ancient Games and Ancient Places* . . . the reason I called it "ancient" was I wanted it to be timeless. In the corridor I had etchings. The plates were later given to the MOMA in the 1960s. I had wood pieces that were placed on a tray and anyone who came in could move them around and compose them. The forms were wood abstract, just like the pieces I use now. They were Cubistic, and they were on a slab and when you came in it was right at the entrance. Here you could create your own compositions.

I wanted basically, in time, to not have sculpture static. I wanted to move around. And have things moving. And also that one person could have many images from one piece if they so wanted it. The "places" were where they traveled. Say that was my hope of going places and playing games. You see, I was going to have a voyage again.

Now the *Royal Voyage of the King and Queen of the Sea* [1956] was a black show. The two central figures, the king and the queen, were the largest pieces—carved wood. But we did have some terra cottas. Those were the gifts. You see, really basically, it has always been first—the form. I wanted to introduce in America very abstract forms, and the only way I could get around it is by calling them gifts—because a gift can be square, it can be a circle, it's unlimited. In *Ancient Games and Ancient Places* there was also a persona of terra cotta with two faces. A male and female face. They were taking trips. And *Black Majesty*, later acquired by the Whitney, was one continent. There were four continents, like the four corners of the earth. I don't remember them all now.

I must say that when I did the first big environmental exhibition *Moon Garden + One*, there was a desk and chairs that belonged to the gallery and I had them moved out. I didn't want a chair or anything to intrude on the environment. So I composed. The walls, the sculpture was on the walls, and it was all black and the window I blocked. That was the first show that blue light

Black Majesty, painted wood, 32″ high, by LN, 1955. *Whitney Museum of American Art*

was used. I didn't block both windows. But I closed *one* window and left the

other open. I framed a whole piece of sculpture by placing it in the window. I
composed the whole thing. It was not really for an audience, it was really for
my visual eye. It was a feast—for myself.

Now it's how many years since the Grand Central? Almost twenty years
ago. From that show until now, look what's happened in the art world:
Abstract Expressionist, Nonobjective, Pop, Conceptual, Earth Works, et
cetera. When you think of that in that time, it made more of an impact than
now, with all the things that have gone on.

My first big wall, *Sky Cathedral*, was installed in MOMA in 1956. It was
upstairs, but it was in a corner and I had dark light. And I even got a pole and
the pole was in front of it to give it different depth and space. That one
line—you buy it, a pole, and it went from top to bottom. And then the wall
came behind it. So you had space . . . and it held it. That one pure line held it.

When Arp came to America and had his one-man show at the Museum of
Modern Art in 1958, the wall, *Sky Cathedral*, was installed on the day of his
opening. Now I never met Arp, but someone told me that he said he looked at
the wall as it was being installed and said, "I will write a poem about this
work. Because it is the façade of America," and he did.

I didn't even know there was an artist by the name of Schwitters until
Arp came and saw my piece and compared it to his work. In principle,
Schwitters wanted total environment. Well, I didn't even know it, so it must
have been in the air. In principle I think there's a kind of parallel thinking, but
it was independent of each other.

Well, you know the world is circular, and many art lovers naturally read
about Arp's poem. And immediately I'd been established. So, you see when
the time came, I must give credit to the great artists in Europe who forced the
hand of the American people, in the art world where it counted. They could
no longer ignore my work.

My whole life's been late. Don't forget, dear, that I was fifty-eight in 1958
when I was in the show at the Museum of Modern Art—"Sixteen Americans."
And they were all much, much younger than I. There are not many surprises
in a life, though, I must tell you, not in my life. Not many surprises.

I somehow for myself feel independent of an audience and independent
of human beings. I stand right here and feel independent. Because my life was
a solo and I can't thank too many people on earth. I'm not even grateful to

Sky Cathedral, wood painted black, 11′ 3½″ x 10′ ¼″, by LN, 1958. *Museum of Modern Art*

Louise Nevelson

Dans le grand univers terne de la nuit
du crépuscule, de l'imagination, à l'éveil
où le coq du réveille-matin chante, les
bibelots-monstres de Louise Nevelson se
promènent.
Voici Paysage Ancien (ancient landscape)
—un paysage fermé par des planches
d'où l'espérance a pu s'enfuir en
démolissant une.
Voici des sacs à papier pleins d'air
des bibliothèques ambulantes d'anachorètes
des muscles à cocons
des cases débordantes de cossons
des casiers à pyramides maniables.
Le réveil à la vie du jour face aux volets,
le contre-jour où tout est perdu fors
l'honneur, la cascade empaïlée, vous éblouissent.
La grille que nous portons en nous
(the inner gate) par laquelle entre et sort
the noble being, the noble personnage.
Où sont les bouteilles grises empliées de
poussière des catacombes?
La valise de la mariée (the wedding chest)
sous le bras, je disparais dans la Cathédrale du Ciel.
Louise Nevelson a un grand-père sans probablement
le connaître, Kurt Schwitters

—Jean Arp
March 1960

Courtesy of Colette Roberts

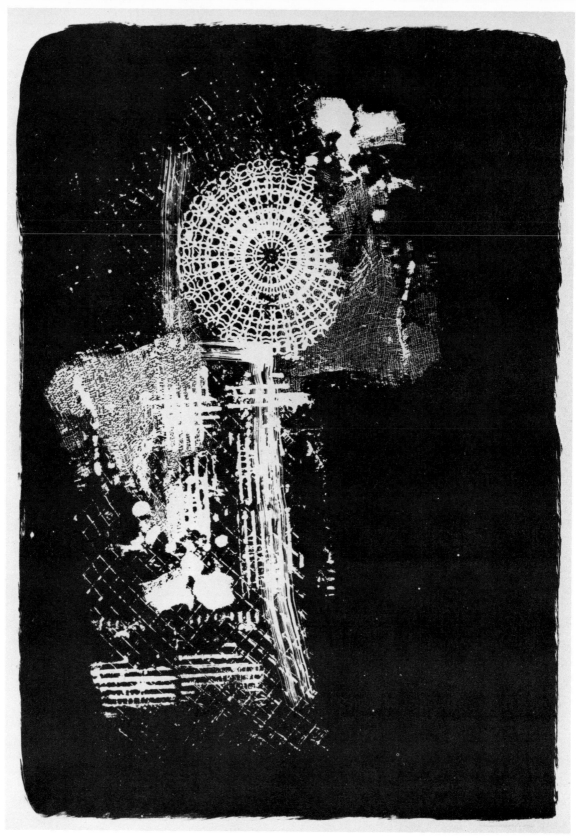

Untitled lithograph, 22″ x 32″, done by LN at Tamarind, 1963.
Whitney Museum of American Art

some people who might think they have helped me. I have no feeling of

"thank you." I feel utterly isolated from that kind of mentality. I could be
modest and say thank you and, oh, yes, and . . . well, I wouldn't bend my
knee one inch if there were not one Jesus Christ but the world was full of
them. This is my life, and I don't permit people to intrude. I take full
responsibility for what I've done and every time I say it I want to cry. That is
true. And that is what gave me my strength and gave me my independence.
And it gave me truly a great deal of sorrow. It's a total price.

I have a good story about Charles Olson from that time. I met Charles
Olson and his wife at an artist's in East Gloucester, and he was a man about six
feet four inches. He had already left Black Mountain College and he came
back to Gloucester to write. So he lived in great poverty. His wife was a
musician and his student, and very attractive. So I would go up there and visit
and he'd come in and he was very friendly. Probably we had met a dozen
times. Then one day when I was beginning to be recognized on a different
level, he came and we were drinking. He wasn't a great drinker—I think I had
more to drink than he. And it was before he spoke, I got the feeling in this
room that a mountain was coming. And sure enough, he let me have it. I was
successful, and so forth. But I felt it like a mountain, a dark cloud. He attacked
me on success. And attacked me and attacked me. So I sat right down in front
of him and I began to cry. I didn't cry because of me. But I cried that I had
looked up to him as a poet and an intelligent thinking man. And he always said
to me that he thought I was one of the very understanding women. And when
he did that, I just broke. And so after that he wrote me notes of apology and so
on, but I felt that . . . I never went back to things once I got that. But the
thing that was interesting was, I went back to visit again and he came to the
door and wanted to talk to me. And I told the hostess not to let him in. So he
left a note. I never saw him after that.

When one gets worldly success, so to speak, recognition, it is as hard to
take success as it is failure. Both pull you out of the center unless the center
matures, grows, and recognizes it. Being a public person requires quite a lot of
things. After all, self-protection. You have to know how to handle it. I think
some pretty good creative minds don't want the responsibility.

For myself . . . it was only after I was established that I didn't feel the
need to pound my head against the wall.

You know, Diana, my first show with Martha Jackson [*Sky Columns Presence*, 1959] after I left Grand Central Moderns was a fulfilling show for me. About that time, I was going to do the white show for Dorothy Miller at MOMA. This was, say, a month or two before. So someone came down to paint boxes black for me. And I had worked and worked on one particular box, and it didn't work. I was so *mad*, I don't do these things any more. But you know, I took a gallon of black paint and *threw it* on the floor. So say one box was as big as twenty-four by thirty-six inches. Depth sixteen inches. And it was stood up (vertically). Well, I picked up the circular piece I was working on and I pushed it, bango, into the box. And I *knew* I had it. The *pièce de résistance*. It was reproduced in the *New York Times*. You see, I got the circle, as big as that—a manhole. *The Sun*. Then a smaller one, I made the second one, now I got the message, and called it *The Moon*.

Now, Diana, think of time. Think of columns. I had built up the height, not Formica but of the same wood, and I built a sort of piece of sculpture by itself. Open-air. Then I would have a dozen columns on it. They were much more impressive then, I must say, than now, because now it's good, but we're used to them. By now it has become my vocabulary. So they don't have the *impact* that was at that time. Anyway Martha had a man, very professional, to come and do the lighting. Now there, we didn't use necessarily all blue (that was at Grand Central Moderns), we used all different fusions of lights, so we broke that.

Dorothy Miller called and invited me to dinner. So I went to dinner, and she asked me if I would be in "Sixteen Americans." I guess I was so taken by storm and surprise about the whole thing—I'd never had an environment there—that without thinking I said that I would do a white show—*Dawn's Wedding Feast*. And that's how it happened. You know, sometimes if you're highly surprised, I think the human mind begins to spark. And when she asked me, in a way it was an homage to her. I had a white wedding cake. A wedding mirror. A pillow. It was a kind of wish fulfillment, a transition to a marriage with the world.

It was already in my mind that I had given myself the title "Architect of Shadow." Then I suppose another thing opened up and I said, "Oh, I'll be an Architect of Light." It's arresting light and arresting shadow, which is fleeting. I take light, which is fleeting, right? But I give it solid substance. I give it architecture.

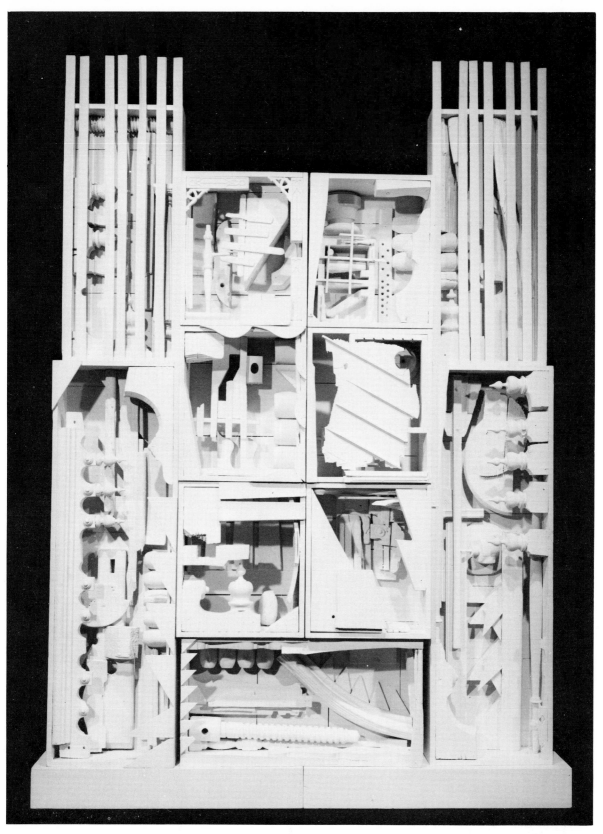

Dawn's Wedding Chapel, wood painted white, 83½″ x 115⅞″, by LN, 1959. *Whitney Museum of American Art*

Dawn's Wedding Feast,
wood painted white,
by LN, 1959.
Museum of Modern Art

If you paint a thing black or you paint a thing white, it takes on a whole different dimension. The white and the black invited different forms. The tones, the weights, are different. See, when I did the work in these colors, I think a state of mind enters into it. And that is enough, because basically this is what has to happen to visual art. Forms have to speak, and color. Now the white, the title is *Dawn's Wedding Feast*, so it is early morning when you arise between night and dawn. When you've slept and the city has slept you get a psychic vision of an awakening. And therefore, between almost the dream and the awakening, it is like celestial. White invites more activity. Because the world is a little bit asleep and you are basically more alive to what's coming through the day.

I feel that the white permits a little something to enter. I don't know whether it's a mood . . . probably a little more light. Just as you see it in the universe. The white was more festive. Also the forms had just that edge. The black for me somehow contains the silhouette, essence of the universe. But I feel that the whites have contained the blacks with a little more freedom, instead of being mood. It moves out a little bit into outer space.

I was hoping, of course, that *Dawn's Wedding Feast* would be kept as a permanent installation in a museum or big concern. That someone would have the vision to buy the entire environment and perhaps enclose it, for instance, on a roof within a glass house and open to the public as a total environment. I would have almost been willing to give it away at the time in order to place it permanently.

Then the gold came after that. Now you see, gold comes out of the earth. It's like the sun, it's like the moon—gold. There's more gold in nature than we give credit for, because every day there are certain reflections where the sun rays hit and you get gold. Every nail we use gives off a light which is almost gold, or silver. Look how many millions of people open cigarette packages. And look, we open this, and look at the light from this paper. It's gold and silver and look how many millions of people are opening this and never see this. That's reflection. That's as pure light as any of the most choice gold and silver in the world.

Gold is a metal that reflects the great sun. And then when you put it on, it's an essence of a so-called reality in the universe. Consequently I think why, in my particular case, gold came after the black and white is a natural. Really I was going back to the elements. Shadow, light, the sun, the moon. If I could speak the way I feel, all these things are in nature, but they symbolize different things. And don't forget that America was considered the land of opportunity. I was asked to be on a panel once and there were rich bankers and someone in the audience asked, "Mrs. Nevelson, how did you happen to pick up old woods on the street?" I said, "Well, I come from the Old Country. I came to Rockland when I was four and a half years old, then I came to New York. And they promised that the streets of America would be paved with gold."

I do think of gold in two ways. One is that the world is shining. Then I also think somewhere there's another element of materialistic quality. I mean it symbolizes so much—the sun and the moon—and somehow, while it comes out of the earth, it's already more sophisticated. It's more that humans have given it something. And you cannot divorce it totally. For instance, we can reverse it. I can say that white is mourning and black is marriage. I can do it consciously. But gold I can't do it. Because the minute you have gold it takes you over. Its splendor. And an abundance. And that abundance is really materialistic.

I think the gold enhanced the forms, enriched them. I loved it. I remember one wall, *Royal Tides* [1961], an exhibition at Martha Jackson's, where the forms were big. It isn't that I felt I explored the gold to the end. The only thing is that there was something in me drawing me to the black. I actually think that my trademark and what I like best is the dark, the dusk. But I've never left anything. That isn't the way I work. I might take up something I was doing twenty years ago, it doesn't matter. The procedure once was that an artist moved from one thing to another. So the first woods I did were in black, then I went into white, then to gold, and so on. Museum people said, "Oh, now, what is going to be your next color?" And I said, "I never left anything." It's true. I don't let anything escape from me. You don't give a thing or throw out a thing. You reorient a thing. If it's necessary that something should come out at a given time, you can take it out. But it isn't destroyed. It's still part of our awareness. You could live a thousand years or even a million and you cannot say that you have finished with a period. I never felt I explored the ultimate black.

When I worked on the white and the gold sculpture, I had two separate studios. One was 41 Spring Street and the other 216 Mott Street. And I worked at the same time in both. There were many reasons for it. The eye gets caught here and here. Now when I worked in the white, I didn't want my eye

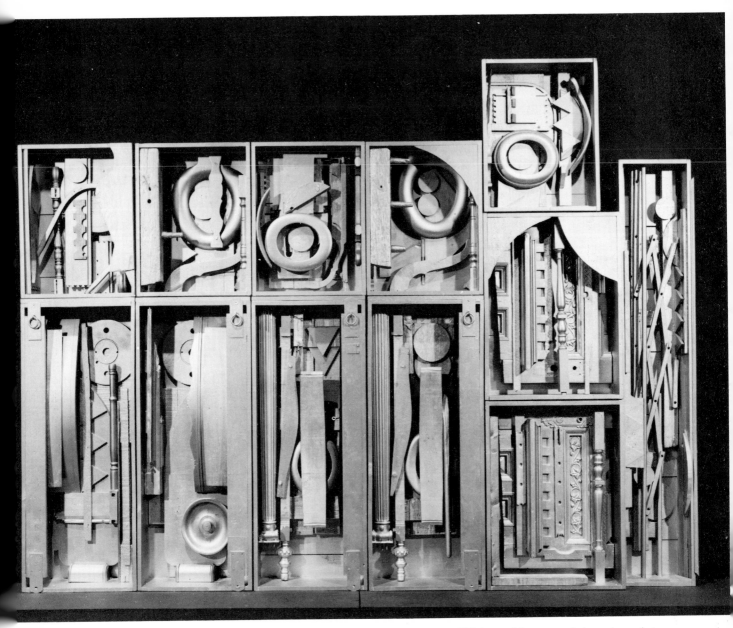

Royal Tide II, painted wood, 126½″ x 94½″, by LN, 1961–63. *Whitney Museum of American Art*

distracted by anything. When I worked on my blacks, I didn't want my blacks or golds detracted from. Because I again wanted total environment. As close as possible to what I was working on. And I think it was great to do it.

*I*n 1962, I was chosen by the Museum of Modern Art to represent the United States government at the Venice Biennale. And I was speechless.

When Dorothy Miller and I left New York and got into Venice, it was a Saturday. I had taken a separate bag with the things that I was going to wear to the reception and parties, my Chinese robes. And I found that Dorothy had her bag, but mine didn't appear. We had changed planes in London and we had heard that very often things would get mixed up because of that change. Now I needed those clothes badly. So I kept asking how long it would be before I could get that bag.

They said, "Oh, maybe in a few days . . ." But my exhibition was opening on Monday and I was getting nowhere fast with them. So finally I said, "Now I'm getting married tomorrow and I've got to have my trousseau. My white wedding dress is in it!" Well, of course I was already sixty-two years old and that was the last thing on my mind. But they got so nervous about this dress and the idea of my getting married that they got busy with wires and calls. And sure enough on Sunday, the bag arrived.

Now the American Pavilion was very old, not too big, and not built for permanency. It had no electricity and depended on natural light. I worked there with the Italian workers and carpenters. I didn't speak any Italian and they didn't speak English. But it was a joy. Because of their efficiency and empathy to compose with me right there. Some of the pieces had been in other shows, the white from parts of *Dawn's Wedding Feast*, much of it from Daniel Cordier, who was then my dealer in Paris. But I composed environments that had never been seen before.

I was given the three large galleries. I painted the entrance room gold, which was circular, so that was the gold environment, first. Then in the two larger galleries, on the right was white, on the left black. I covered the glass ceilings, which were like skylights, with material the color of each environment.

Even before it was open to the public, a woman dealer from Paris came into the gallery while Giacometti was there. She had never seen anything used that way. So she asked Giacometti how he felt about my work, because to her, it didn't seem like sculpture. Not in the conventional sense. And he went to great lengths to explain to her how it was sculpture, and that it was a new form. He was very pleased with it. And my coming there and creating a whole new space appealed to him.

Giacometti, whom I got to know and adored, won the first prize in the exhibition that year, which was fine with me. "Always the bridesmaid, never the bride."

We were coming back from one of the islands next to Venice after a party. It was about four in the morning and the city was still dark . . . and the dawn was just beginning to break, so that those islands with the great cathedrals were darker than the light. It was so perfect, if I can use the word there, as I had ever seen on earth.

I have traveled more, I think, than I ever thought I would, but it has always pertained to art and the work. I have had shows all over the world. South America, Europe, the Mideast, to name a few. My latest trip, in 1975, the State Department sent me to Iran, India, and Japan. You could say that I'm international. I don't have a boundary line. But in a sense I really don't want to travel at all. I don't need that much geography.

I feel that we humans have measurements within ourselves. When I stretch my arms out and up, as I am doing now, I feel I have crossed many times across the ocean and touched all parts of the world. That's why I think the greatest thing we have is the awareness of the mind. Because there we can build many mansions, there we have all the things that are not given to us on earth.

Everyone wants to be winged and fly. They want freedom and I think that's right. But real freedom is freedom of the spirit. In the beginning of your life, you have to go, you have to experience. But eventually, you come back to the self, and what you have inside, you project. The eye is in constant awareness, and it's a projection.

I can sit right here, in the dining room of 29 Spring Street, and look out the window at the enormous school building across the street and see hundreds of windows, with the sunset reflected on them like molten gold across the surface. Then the moon will come over and give it another light. Then the windows at night would be totally black, and one window with one tiny light will appear. And one window that has a blacker area from the glass that is broken makes a perfect composition. For me. These are the keys to my existence.

The American Pavilion at the Venice Biennale: LN, Giacometti, and Dorothy Miller in front of the white environment. *Maryette Charlton*

Entrance room to American Pavilion, gold environment. *Maryette Charlton*

Dorothy Miller and LN setting up the galleries. *Maryette Charlton*

LN, early 1960s. *Diana MacKown*

My voyages have been in my work and in my so-called reality. I have the world, right here, "in my own backyard." And truly I don't need anything else. There is so much work to be done that I can move an inch and circle the world.

I've done sculpture, paintings, drawings, graphics, everything visual. Now even the collages. I brought in natural wood, colored glass, old etchings. They are kind of essences that were demanding the ultimate of a line or the ultimate of a color, ultimate of texture. I've covered so many facets.

I have given shadow a form. And I gave reflection a form. I used glass for reflections, then I used mirror. Now we know that shadow and reflection, in a way, have a form—but not really an architectural or sculptural form. But one can do that. So I consider that I am an architect of shadow, and I'm an architect of reflection. Those are titles I gave to myself. Then the Plexiglas. There you have a transparent material, which gives us the ultimate of light.

So in my kind of thinking, which includes reflection, which includes opaque, which includes the rest period, which includes the activity, naturally the mind was constantly restless. Searching for that one line that would hold everything. And that line may just be a dot. Why not? You finish a sentence and you just take your pen or pencil . . . you make a dot. And look what it does to the mind! It arrests that place. And that's what I do in my work.

The artist has the equipment to manipulate life in a particular way. If it's visual. We talk about the nerve ends. But in us, in this machinery, there's a thing that centers, just a dot, where we are aware of the livingness of our lives. We were born with it, but we had to clean away the forms of so-called reality—of the outside world. And we in its place, in a way, build our world.

The deeper you go into the self, the more you recognize who you are, and only when you do can you project. I think there's something very important about character: character is structure. Character is the architecture of the being. And once you go into the inner being, you will find that everything you encompass, in any direction you choose, is your own.

First, I don't think many people would dig that far if there weren't other complexes. I think that what's very interesting in my life is the fact that in the history of time, I should have had an easier life. By appearance. By my surroundings. Then what happened that I didn't conform? Maybe nature played a part in it. There are certain biological things that you start with. For example, when you see a person with an enormous drive, you'll see something in them that is excessive. There's an abundance of something to overcompensate some other things. Abundance has something to do with it. That's the one ingredient. Second, drives, even my own, so I'm not dismissing it, are built on lacks. Nature, it overbalances you in one thing, and it takes something away from you. You can only conceive of drives when there are great negatives within one's life. It is a night. And then you *have* to fight for the day. And the darker it is, the further your drives.

I have had great highs in my life, I have had great lows. And you become sensitized. That's not necessarily in the seeing. It can be of the feeling. The basic thing, I think, for having lived at all is the greater awareness. And that awareness added and added and added. Things that blinded you and the things that angered you to the point of almost insanity.

My eyes have been my awareness. When you think, in my creative life, well, say at least fifty-odd years, and the daily living like that, can you conceive of the accumulation of awareness in a visual direction?

By the mid-sixties I had reached the unfolding in myself to recognize that there are only a few notes that give me my structure. Beethoven took the octave, eight notes, and he built a world of sound. For myself, I didn't need eight notes. I reduced it. I took two notes and I built my world. Now in my own kind of thinking, I've already established that there isn't a thing outside of us that we haven't within us. Everything that has been produced on the earth, or the minerals under the earth, is contained within the human being, in our bodies and minds. We carry locomotion by our movement. We carry the structure, our bodies. We stand on two feet, and we are vertical. So in my work I use the principle of the vertical and the horizontal—two lines. That is what I call the skeleton, the structure. And on that structure I can elaborate, or I can leave it in a natural state. The structure holds.

Once you have that fundamental key, you are in control to move into almost anything. I can work on a large scale or a small scale. There's no difference to me in that sense. I have, oh, I don't know how many works that are inch by inch, they're so tiny, and then I have great big Cor-ten works that are sometimes forty feet in height. Size and scale is not the ultimate. It's the essence. You can make a little thing a few inches small, but let's assume it's a mountain. It truly looks enormous. It has been said that a great dancer can dance within a cubic inch and contain a universe.

You know, Diana, it's easier for me to talk about my shows in the past.

Untitled collage, 18″ x 24″, by LN, 1975, photographed in studio. *Diana MacKown*

Living room, 29 Spring Street, New York City, 1965. *Diana MacKown*

Living room, house on 30th Street, New York City, 1950s. *Jeremiah W. Russell*

Now, in the sixties and seventies, there have been so many shows of my work, not only in New York but all over the world. At one time, an artist sometimes didn't even show for ten years but now things are geared up to such a momentum that I can hardly keep track of them. One of the great joys is to know that the Whitney Museum has so much of my work. And I intend to give them more. I love that museum. First, it is truly *the* American museum. Secondly, I came in on the ground floor, literally. When the building of the new Whitney was completed in 1967, I had the first retrospective of my work there, so naturally that was very important to me. Now that show was very meaningful to me. It covered the complete fourth floor of the museum and greatest space, in a way, of the museum. So I was making an enormous environment which would hold that space together. Now creating the *Rain Forest* for the restrospective was, in a way, the highlight of the show. I had a narrow space that was like a hallway constructed and the walls were painted black. So when the elevator would come up to the fourth floor, people were drawn to walk through this passageway. In a way, it was like a bridge, you might say the corridor was an environmental bridge to the rest of the show. It was completely dark, just a few lights, so that the Plexiglas sheets hung between the open frame boxes to catch and reflect the light. Then I had moons hanging from the ceiling and pieces coming up from the floor. Then there was a white wall, *New Continents*, on a very high base, to the left of the *Rain Forest*, so that the wall looked as if it were at a distance. *Sky Cathedral* from MOMA could be seen at the further end of the tunnel. And of course there were my pieces on loan from museums all over the world, such as the Tate in London, an enormous gold wall that was my gift to the British people, and the huge black wall *Homage to Six Million* series.

Early landscapes in wood, drawing from the thirties, some plaster and terra cotta. Oil paintings. A bit later in the early fifties the etchings and pieces of that period, leading up to my big walls, like *Sky Cathedral* from the Museum of Modern Art, done in the later fifties. Then of course there were the metal pieces, *Atmosphere and Environment* series, Plexiglas pieces. Black environments, gold environments, and white environments. So that the range and amount of work that these pieces encompassed was the total universe.

I have never been enslaved by the lack of space. Every space seems to have something limited about it. Either the ceilings are too low, or the rooms too confining. Or it can be the general architecture of the building itself. So

Installation photograph, Whitney retrospective, 1967.
Whitney Museum of American Art

Rain Forest Columns, painted wood, 133½″ high, by LN, 1962–67. *Whitney Museum of American Art*

Photograph of LN taken for catalogue by John Gordon, Louise Nevelson retrospective, Whitney Museum, 1967. *Diana MacKown*

that is why I usually and always had, way back, put on my own shows. And there is always, through working this way—total involvement, that the accumulation of all the works make a unity that corresponds to the same action as creating one piece of work. So you have one body of work. And then something enters in the physical activity itself of composing right on the spot that gives a great vitality to the work. So I always have a choice to move things around. To add and subtract. At the last minute to have a "brainstorm" like a bolt of lightning to place a piece in a certain way that would give that particular environment a whole new dimension. So it's the immediacy of a given situation.

A few years ago I was asked to show in the Houston Museum. Well, everyone warned me that I would have a hard time because we were having the new wing, which was Mies van der Rohe, and there would be the glare of glass and all. But they covered all of the space that was the windows with black material. And the people that worked there were fine and the lighting was professionally done and I still consider that one of the great shows. Because there was just my white work as you entered—frontal. It was nothing to do with the rest, the rest was black wood. It was carefully planned and the lights were right. Then it dawned on me that the Arts Club in Chicago, where I also had a show, was done by Mies van der Rohe, and this. Now, I can't explain why my work looked so well in his space. I still can't.

Then in contrast, I had a show in Paris at the Rothschild mansion, C.N.A.C. That was an old building and it was so impressive in its own way, having two marble staircases and two griffons in the front and then this façade between, all the elaborate work. They had their own kind of sculpture around, really, and then they had these things above the banister and it was quite something to confront. Now, I didn't want the work to be placed like decoration, so I clustered these black metal columns, different sizes, on different bases asymmetrically right in the front entrance. I still feel it was right to do. And it proved to me that the work can be placed in architecture of different periods and it holds its own.

That pleased me, actually. Because I had seen it first in America at the Walker Art Center, which was built by Ed Barnes. It was just marvelous because the building is built for works of my kind. I mean it was contemporary and great. Then, as we moved from there to San Francisco, there, the museum was old. It was a modern museum but in an older building, and it stood up rather well. It was interesting that the building had a two-story ceiling and I thought that these walls might get lost in that upper space. But no, that wasn't true. There's something about the human scale that sees it eye level and doesn't really drift too far.

Now we'll jump back and forth a little, Diana. We opened again in America, Dallas, and it was again an old building. Actually, it was broken up a great deal with columns, marble columns, and I think in one way it was the hardest because there were not only marble columns, it has a balcony. It's open space, but the space is encumbered with these columns and the balcony banister and big doors so that you don't have one room that you close off. So we did the best we could. And again I think the work stood up.

I jump around and people say, oh, why does she have to go there so much to her openings? I can't go to every exhibition but I make a selection. Well, I have learned so much. I prefer to spend my energies that way than in other ways. When I went with these shows, I learned a great deal about how these things are placed. And how they hold their own. I learned and I really got quite an insight into various spaces, the architectural, the ornamental, just everything about architecture and the work that's in it.

I have seen sculpture placed and misplaced. When I was on a panel not too long ago in Newport, Rhode Island, there were several large pieces of sculpture that were placed around. But they weren't placed with any kind of awareness in the environment, so the effect of much of it was a hodgepodge. And the works of art did not necessarily hold up well. In fact in some cases, they destroyed each other. So that now, particularly, that we have and can produce these monumental pieces, I think that room must be made for people who really have to study and make a blueprint for the placement of sculpture in space. Maybe we could call them sculpture-architects.

Remember I was in my early seventies when I came to the monumental, outdoor sculpture. Now something in the living conscious being has a beat, and you move on. Something happens and you become private, something happens and you become public. Sometimes you want to be alone, sometimes you want to communicate. And that is expressed in the work. Now from the time that I did work in the so-called round—in the forties, the war years, and early fifties—I had begun wanting to enclose it. My whole work in wood was enclosure, an enclosed or interior environment. Then I began breaking a little deeper. I was getting to want more and more enclosure, and consequently I

Work in progress, plastic pieces with black wooden forms, 29 Spring Street. *Diana MacKown*

Transparent Sculpture VI, Plexiglas, 20″ x 19″, by LN, 1967–68. Whitney Museum of American Art

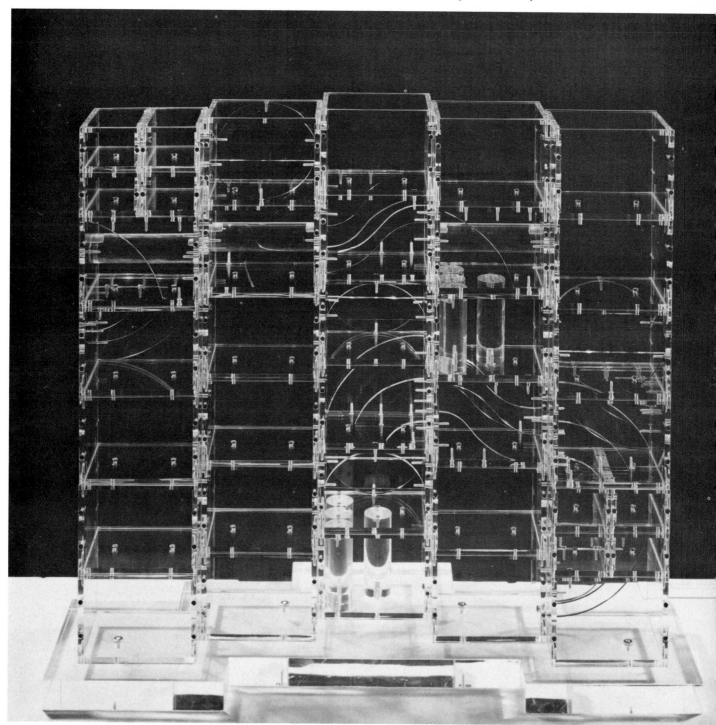

Transparent Horizon, Cor-ten steel painted black, 20′ high, by LN, 1975. *Diana MacKown*

used glass in front of them. It became more mysterious and deeper in and the glass gave it another texture. For myself, I felt that I wanted to embrace it more and more and not expose.

So then I naturally wanted the next step, and I moved into what I called the out-of-doors sculpture. I had been through the enclosures of wood, I had been through the shadow. I had been through the enclosure of light and reflection. And now I was ready to take away the enclosures and come out into the open and let the out-of-doors be the reflection.

Diana, you know the new piece that has just been placed in Boston, *Transparent Horizon* [1975]? Twenty feet high, Cor-ten, at MIT. I like that piece as well as I ever liked any of my public pieces. The placement of the piece is right in its environment. Let me explain. Number one, there's a black piece of Calder's that was purchased about ten years ago. Now you can't see the Calder from my piece. You have to walk around the I. M. Pei building to see his and vice versa. But if you go upstairs in the new building, which is only four stories high, you can see the Calder there and my piece on the other side. They are complementary. And I think they both hold. To my kind of thinking, mine is feminine and the other is not. But that's a point of view. Calder's is more rounded and mine is taller and vertical. Mine has a kind of play. It's monumental. But it isn't regimented. There are two "personages." The small figure is the female and the tall one is the male. Not a man or a woman. But the male principle and the female principle.

It's twenty feet in height and almost looks the height of the building. Then it's formal. Formal and playful. It stands like this door, straight and frontal. Then you look over the Charles River and you see the big building like Hanover that faces you. Then the sidewalk becomes a pattern to enclose the piece. So you don't see it standing isolated, you see it extending. At this point the trees are no taller than the piece and are very delicate. There isn't one big branch.

Then there are lights that are placed in the entrances of the buildings and they're not too prominent. So the environment becomes its frame.

I think often people don't realize the meaning of space. Space, they think, is something empty. Actually, in the mind and the projection into this three-dimensional world, space plays the most vital part in our lives. Your concept of what you put into a space will create another space. I have seen a person walk in a room and dominate the space. Space has an atmosphere, and what you put into that space will color your thinking and your awareness. The whole body is in space. We are space.

I've lived in so many places in my life, and I've never lived in an environment that was totally to my liking. My house isn't what I have chosen. It really isn't what I would choose. But it's where I live. And there hasn't been a space that I've lived in that I didn't transform into an environment for myself. Either by placement of objects, or colors, or tearing out an area to open a space. I love an empty house. I love the luxury of space.

You know, I have been a collector all my life. You name it, I have collected it. Not once, but many times. I was in my early thirties when I started buying Eilshemius's paintings, and altogether I must have had over one hundred. One very important one I gave to the Whitney Museum many years ago. I have placed what I have collected in museums as best I could. Marvelous American Indian pottery that I collected all over this country when nobody even paid any attention to them. African sculpture. Countless silver, pewter. Chinese lacquers. Other artists' work. For a minute I had a Paul Klee. Rugs, antique furniture, samplers, the Mexican Santos, laces. Everything that my eye valued I would veer to. I collect for my eye. It's an awareness. A feast for the eye. A banquet for the eye. The wonder of collecting is that you are constantly in training to look for that added dimension that you identify with. That kind of energy search is very living. I have learned more through my collections, say, handling old lace that I have used in my first etchings, than any formal training could give me.

Objects that one collects have vibrations, and they can usurp you. So I didn't always like to have things around me. But I love the activity of accumulating them. I am still giving things away and I am still collecting because that is an activity I understand and it's a natural. Artists are born collectors.

Once someone came to my house and looked in a huge Formica closet that I had built into the wall, full of china, pewter, crystal, silver. And they said, "Louise, what do you need all these things for?" I said, "I don't need them, I want them."

Think of placing objects in a space. The size of them, the forms of the pieces, and the color. That is the physical thing. But what about the inner being? The atmosphere. When you sit down and you're *in* the right place. The effect and reaction to ourselves—or when you eat from a certain plate. It can

29 Spring Street, late 1960s. *Diana MacKown*

be just a so-called ordinary plate or a very precious plate. But if an object is in its right place, it's enhanced to grandeur. More than that, it pleases the inner being and that, I think, is very important. That equals harmony.

Now I don't mean taste, because truly, taste is out as such. That is a nineteenth-century concept. And good taste has never really been defined. The effort of projecting "good taste" is so studied that it offends me. No. I prefer to negate that. We have to put a period to so-called good taste. We have to get into placement of structure in environment.

People usually think of their own environment. They belong to a little community, they hold certain so-called beliefs. And they live within it, they dress within it, they eat within it. They put a little notch in their belt and they think that they have arrived. They don't get a scope that the whole world is theirs if they can encompass it. They don't move out into not only a universal concept, which is limited, but a celestial . . . into all the planets and all the stars.

Let me say this. I think we have reached another age. I think people will have to begin to think entirely differently. I've often thought that maybe the fine arts, as we know them, are a thing of the past. Now I, for one, would still like to think that art for art's sake is great. I think that's where art is. But what is considered fine art now is what could become, sort of, the folk art of the future. Technology, really, is still in its infancy. The potential of technology. If you're aware of what's taking place in our time, the new materials that technology has introduced are changing the way of thinking. They're taking it out of one kind of thing and taking it into another. The world as such—technology, science, chemistry—has opened avenues, and we, if we are centered, can move with it. We take all of these things and we add something of our own awareness. The point is, you take that material and you stamp on it your own consciousness.

In our times, the new materials like Plexiglas or Cor-ten are just a blessing for me. Because I was ready for them and the material was ready for me. Consequently, every day of my life parallels my creativity. There's something about it that's one. Take the materials of the big industrialists like the Du Ponts. Now great fortunes were spent in a commercial way, to accumulate more fortunes. They did it for commerce. But then the artist comes along and is ready to use that. Myself, I came along and I recognized that it is not only Lucite.

It's not only that I take something. Look at the minds through the ages to project this material into the world. The greatest minds had to produce it, the greatest scientists, the greatest chemists gave us this material. And they have introduced another dimension, where we can enter into another place. And so, when I'm working with my materials, I recognize that they are accumulation of thought. Cor-ten, Plexiglas, all materials are accumulation of thought.

So by the time you are ready for a thing, don't underestimate that there are other minds that are ready for you. For instance, I have been going now, for several seasons, to Lippincott's, the foundry up in North Haven. And when I go to the foundry to work, the whole place is at my disposal. It is geared for the artist to work. With materials, with the men who assist me. I can work from six in the morning to as late at night, with as many assistants as I need for as many days as I wish. It is set up to accommodate the artist in a whole environment. So it's just great!

I started with aluminum. And I'd make my sculpture, I call them sculpture-collage. I would compose and the men would work with me—direct. And eventually I noticed that there was a great deal of Cor-ten steel lying around. At first I felt, oh, that metal, I can't work with it. It's impossible, it's so strong. But I got used to being in the foundry, and in the meantime I had already gotten acquainted with how to use aluminum. I knew if I wanted a half-circle, they would put it through a machine and in a few seconds, you get it. Now the longer I went up, the closer I got acquainted with this material Cor-ten, and after a few years, which means last year really, I said that I'd like to try it. I did try it, and I found that I must have been ready for it. Because it was no such thing as a challenge. I found that in my hands and in my way of thinking at this point, it was almost like butter—like working with whipped cream on a cake.

I was using steel as if it was ribbon made out of satin. And somehow it gave me another dimension. It gave me the possibility of maybe fulfilling the place and space and environment that I have probably consciously, unconsciously, been seeking all my life.

I start on the basis that reality is a shift. For instance, I just came from a trip in an airplane, and, all right, I saw the clouds under me. Well, when I was a little girl we grew up thinking God was above the clouds! Now I think the revolution of humans going up into space is so important, because it has given us a new map of the world. A whole new map that was never dreamt of. When

LN at Lippincott's, among the aluminum "trees." *Diana MacKown*

Pace to Tonys — 1975

mikes

1.„ ☐ boxes with doors (unpainted)

2.„ ☐   "   "   "   "

3.„ ▱ "

4.„ ⑤ Walls

5.„ ⑫   "

6.„ 1 Standing piece ▯ banister

7.„   metal (Illuminar)
          pieces
          Lippincott
          June 17-18 - 1975

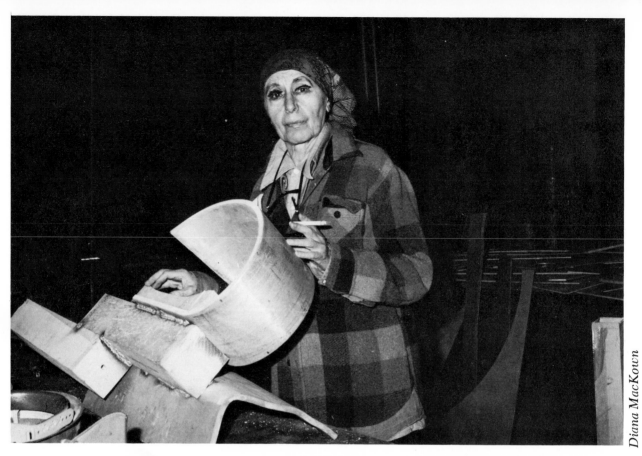

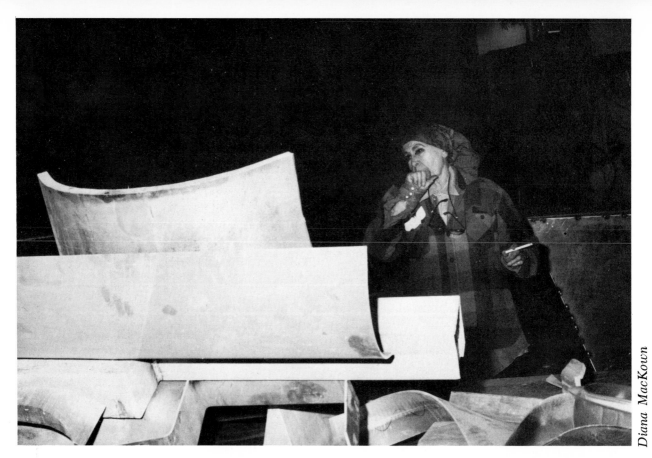

you get a whole new map and you recognize it, then you see the shift of every thought that we have ever had.

So if you can live in the present, recognize the past, and project a bit into where we're going, that's great. And my recognition of this is that when I am working, I know that I am working back into time, through all civilizations, and so it gives me a whole foundation where my back can *really* move. The Indians used to take a bow and arrow. They would go back against that back and when they shot the arrow, they would lean back. We, Western civilization, think you have to lean forward. But truly, the Orientals and the Indians that are in their hunk of thinking recognize that the further *back* they could go, the speedier and swifter they went forward. And so, by the same token of thought and understanding, when I'm working with the materials I recognize that Cor-ten steel like any other material is accumulation of thought.

There are laws we have to concede are standing in step with our time: light and dark, day and night, time and space, the laws of gravity and weight. And since we have them, I use them. Maybe some time from now they will not be needed or necessary any longer. But they are apparently necessary to us at our present time of consciousness.

But the thing is, the time may come, with computers, with technology, when humans will not need this manifestation, this projection into three dimensions. Even in sacred books, like the Indian philosophies, they don't feel—as long as you are laboring and working—that's the height. It's the place of contemplation, you see, that is where you don't have to make anything or do anything. But I, for my own needs, prefer to play the game with awareness, on earth, three-dimensionally. It's a choice I've made. I could easily have moved into an area of meditation and contemplation, and that is higher according to all philosophers. But I claim physical activity teaches me so much. My feeling is that there is great intelligence in labor. When I get up in the morning and open my eyes, I know that I am breathing. And that is already so living—I move from that place. That living awareness moves me as I move it to an activity that encompasses the mind, the body, and the total consciousness. So I feel that I could not have projected my world only through contemplation. Since I *did* want to project a three-dimensional world for myself, it could not have been done without physical activity.

I built my empire. Now I use the word in a way that is very personal for

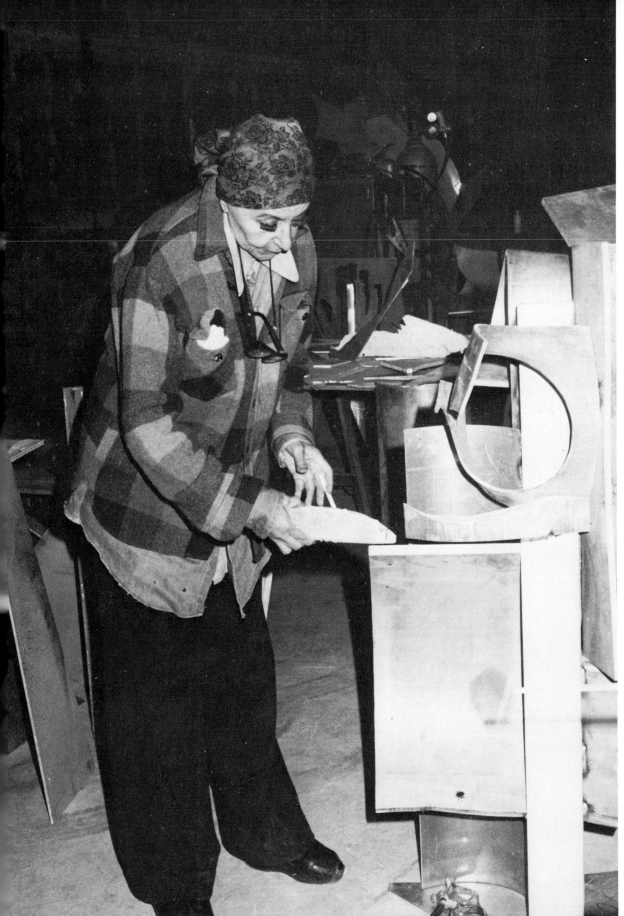

myself. I mean an empire of aesthetics, and that is the true empire for me, and it's never limited and you never finish. It is a personal empire of recognition.

I say I built my empire, and in a way I did. But on the other hand, the mirror out there has reflected, to me, a totality.

I think I'm a social being. I like people and I like having people around me. Friends have given me the feeling of respect for the work, understanding. But I feel that people are the extension of the self, that's why I appreciate them. Other people are a reflection of my awareness. I need them, of course. I would go insane if I didn't have people around me, because if you have no communication with anybody but yourself, it's impossible. I think that originality is the artist's prerequisite, but no one is *totally* original. The human mind that would push to that place of originality would go mad. You have to communicate. But you must also think that in communicating you are communicating almost totally with yourself.

Some years ago I used to go into a certain bar and it had mirrors on the wall, and the mirrors were so constituted that you saw infinite reflections of the same image. If I was looking in the mirror, I would see countless reflections of myself. When I am with people and when I communicate, it is almost like a reflection, in that same sense. There may be a million reflections and a million people reflecting, but I am the one who is reflecting myself.

When you are centered, people can't control you because they are your reflection. By the same token, you are their reflection. The people that I've communicated with, had I not done so, would have left me a little less rich. And there hasn't been a movement in art that hasn't given me a wider spectrum. I feel, in a way, that my work has encompassed every movement. I started with Cubism and I've gone through every period. It was not my desire to consciously do that. But it was like a tree that grew. It unfolded. So I feel that in the end, I have used a hunk of time.

I don't know of any movement in art in my lifetime that did not have its importance. I don't negate any of it. But of course there are the great crescendos. I feel that we walk in and out of green pastures. Music has its fortissimos and it has its rest periods, and in some ways I feel that we are sort of quiet at this period. It seems to me that humanity has been taxed by governments, and the wars and problems. And so the human energies and

LN outside at Lippincott's, 1975. *Diana MacKown*

emotions have become sort of spent. In nature the trees have their winter, and don't forget that when the leaves are gone, that tree is *not dead*. The tree is getting ready for the next period.

In our times, people are in search. The soul is in search, probably more than ever. I think that there is a great search, almost abnormally so, for art. People want something that is creation. They need the artist to create for them. Where people used to maintain in the past, that art was decoration, we now know that art is a communication with life. I think society wouldn't exist without the creative mind. We have to keep going back to this; I think creation is the source, the reason people are alive and living. In their minds they're holding onto it, feeding on it. That is why they are willing to buy things today. They are paying for creation and communicating with creation. That is their way of communicating with a living thing.

America is a young country, and in the history of art we must applaud America. Because in the forties, fifties, sixties, and seventies, we did something in art that no country did in such a short span. I don't know how many museums, but hundreds of museums have come up. Almost every college and university has its own beautiful museum. And that goes from Maine to California, east coast to west coast. They get the greatest architects. And they're teaching art history in every school. Consequently, this whole land has blossomed. I don't know of any other big land that ever blossomed so fast and so well. I'm sitting here in the seventies, and there is a difference between the forties and the seventies like thousands of years in any other time in history. We cut time so fast. So I'm sitting here in the same place, right in New York City, fifty-five years now and being prolific to begin with. And things are coming now to me which I never dreamt. It isn't that I'm in a different position. But the times have changed. Let me put it this way. In the past people went to California—there was a gold rush. And now my mind in a way has reached a place where there is this rush coming in, this rush of great creative energy. My mind is a gold mine.

So we have our colleges and schools and museums. All the wonderful things that are being given to us. But like everything else, there are two sides to the coin.

You know, in the art world, we have the same things the politicians have. It is not as free and easy as we think. We have a few who have controlled the artist's thinking and that have even held the brushes for the artist. So you can see how unfortunate that is. In the art world it's so sacred that no one would think of criticizing certain people. They're like kings. Most artists are afraid they'll be blackballed behind the scene, and they're pretty intimidated. Well, that isn't for me. My life's been tough and I still fight it. I managed without their help, so to hell with them. But what I resent about this is I feel that we are permitting these monsters to control the cultural life, and how many people and their children's children are going to be touched by this? It's a great danger. And the greatest danger is that creation gets a little intimidated and the artist readjusts to the norm. The artist no longer moves from his or her center but permits a monster to intrude. That kind of success is mediocrity right away. Any creative act on earth must come from that person who is doing it.

There is something about the projection that has an essence that you can't quite find on earth. I take it out of the action of the universe and give it that other action. That's why people call *my* work mysterious. I look back now—every step [knocking wood] of the way back—and I see what I saw all the time. I think I'm very aware of the present—time. Those are the necessities. But I really have never been quite here on earth. And I'm glad of it. Maybe the whole thing is an illusion or a mirage. If you're going to see that the world is made out of concrete and stone, totally—you're blocked. But if you see the world in transparency, you can move and there is nothing to block you.

I have taken everything out of this world, everything that I could, to become more aware of what it is. Let me explain something that happened in San Francisco not too long ago. Evidently they had read a few things about me, and someone who was at the luncheon party said to me, "Mrs. Nevelson, we hear or we read that when you eat raisins, you make a selection of each raisin . . ." and the article ended up saying, what a trivial thing. Well, you see that the party that quoted it was so limited that they didn't penetrate the whole thing. When you are eating raisins—I haven't eaten them for twenty years but never mind—why shouldn't I select every little form that I put in my mouth? Now I would say that that's one of the basic things I'm pleased about in retrospect . . . that twenty or thirty years ago when I probably didn't have anything else but raisins, or a package of raisins, I made a selection of each one. I gave each little form its due. I didn't fill my mouth with a *bunch* of raisins. *That* would offend me. Now I think that is more important to state and give people to think about than a lot of subjects that I couldn't talk about in history books, even art and architecture. I love art and architecture, and I know there are critics and authorities that can certainly surpass me, because it means a life study to really be authoritative. But when I put a raisin in my mouth I know what I'm doing.

What I would like to think I had was a personal, maybe an original, let's say I had my own way of seeing situations. Situations are very architectural. They have a form. They have a place and they have a time. That's more than special, it's important. Because I feel that everything we do on the exterior is an extension of our image consciousness. I don't think it's just a façade that you project. Really you're not projecting for anyone, you're fulfilling your own image. So all these things, if they are realized, become your architecture.

I observe for myself as you know that I'm really a good house cleaner. Well, when I clean house or sweep the street in front of the house, I am not really cleaning house. I am building architecture. Every time, because the way I place a thing back, the way I touch a thing, the way I move a thing . . . so for me it is exercise in space of building a beautiful architecture. And if I can, why not live in it?

You know I am constantly picking things up and getting on my knees. I'm seventy-six. I will get on my knees and wipe up a floor or the stairs. I can go through those four flights in the house in twenty minutes. Now for me, it is just not cleaning. When I have a cleaning woman or man, they do it to make the house clean. I do it for a higher order.

Same thing when I put myself together or create something to wear. I love to put things together. My whole life is one big collage. Every time I put on clothes, I am creating a picture, a living picture, for myself. Truly, I am caught probably in clothes, to my way of thinking, at the turn of the century. I like clothes that are upholstered. I like that you build up your clothes, and build up, and even the hat. You can do it two-dimensionally, you can do it three-dimensionally, and every time I do it, when I go back to my work, I use that again.

When I went to the warehouse, now, I didn't want to wear anything that I couldn't mess up. I had a red skirt that was an Indian squaw skirt that I got in Albuquerque some years ago. Then I put on a blue denim, washed-out jacket. And then there was a belt, it's red, it's leather, it's red and tan, and I

put it around my neck like a necklace. Then I put one of those laboring kerchiefs around my head. Blue, I think. I created a harmony. If anyone'd seen me, I was dressed, according to my dimension. By the same token that I use my eyes, I don't want to offend those that I communicate with. You don't have to do less, even if you're scrubbing floors; you can still do it with harmony.

I feel the clothes that I have worn all my life have been freedom, a stamp of freedom—because I've never conformed to what is being worn. I remember once in the 1950s . . . I was working very hard at the time and I was living in that lovely house on East 30th Street. So I remember that I would wear, say, a black dress, but I always loved beautiful laces, so I had jackets out of beautiful laces. And black hats. So this man used to take me out and take me to all the night clubs and the smart places. He'd always comment on girls that were coming into these night clubs. The skirt was too short, the shoes didn't match, all of that. And I always thought that I dressed special, at least for my kind of thinking, and rather simple. What can you do with black and white? And finally, one day, it struck my sense of humor—we were sitting in a big night club right here over the Washington Bridge, where people gambled for high stakes. And finally I turned around and said, "What do you think of my clothes?" And he said, "Dear, *shmattes. Shmattes*" (rags). Well, I looked down and from his point of view, naturally the lace jacket was an antique and was old, so to him, I suppose it did look like rags.

So I never conformed in that sense. But on the other side, in the past, way in the past, artists were always to look poor in America. And they couldn't go into fashion. An artist friend of mine, a painter, said she had her mother's diamond bracelets in the bank and a mink coat, and she said, "I wouldn't be *seen* among artists dressed like that." Why make such a distinction? Isn't it really terribly conventional to think you have to be in a mold? To present a certain thing? Well, I broke that. Let's break tradition. That's exactly why I dress the way I do. Since I have such esteem for the creative mind, I wanted to really open the door. I felt that nothing was too good for anybody if they could recognize it.

I love old robes. I think I was the first person to wear a sixteenth-century Mandarin Chinese robe on top of a blue denim work shirt. Years ago. I still have it and I still do it.

Now I have a shawl that I have had for years, a paisley I paid very little

for in Maine, and I decided to have a chinchilla coat made. So I reversed the concept of that. I had the chinchilla put inside and the paisley outside, to make a statement for myself that there is no difference in matter, as such.

I'm a great believer in a person who presents themselves, not too consciously, but that they feel right about their appearance. And they come already with that asset of feeling right. I don't mean that you have to be expensively dressed. It's nice to be informal, it's nice to be formal. I don't see why we have to go to either extreme. There's a place where people are people and confront other people, with dignity and all the niceties that we humans are capable of. But the point is, when I go to a party or I'm invited someplace, I project something. For me clothes and presentation of self is a projection of a total personality.

I recall that I went to a party once. Now it was the Bar Association and my lawyer was in it. And I thought since it was my lawyer, and there were going to be people of that sort, I'll still wear all the trimmings, but I'll play it down a little bit. And I did. And when I got there I couldn't speak. I was a lady. And that wasn't the role. Life is a stage and I couldn't speak. And I was so unhappy because I couldn't project anything. And I decided to hell with that. I couldn't speak, and I understood Charlie Chaplin.

I don't use anything else: only my eyes. I don't feel dressed without my eyelashes. I don't wear one pair . . . I glue several pairs together and then put them on. I like it and it's dramatic, so why not?

Personally, I'm dramatic, it seems. I like a whole thing, a formal thing—not clothes that show every part of the body and almost naked. I have a feeling maybe my appearance is deceptive. Because if you're going to put on a show like I do, they don't know beneath that façade there's something else. You don't love a person. You love their position and their possessions . . . if you take away and strip that person to the naked self I don't think there'd be much love, unfortunately. We're caught just the same. Suppose, take me at my age and I didn't have a reputation and this or that and the other. I'd just be an old woman in a corner. And I'll tell you what I'd be doing . . . my chair would be toward the wall so no one could see me and I couldn't see them. Why should I be naked before everyone? Let me put it this way, dear, in life you cannot dig for the truth in every area. Must there be an answer? You take a flower, and you take every petal, and you won't have a flower. Keep the flower.

I respect nature, because it has a way of tying up your life. Nature is the intelligence because somehow it rights your life, both ways: RIGHT and WRITE. But at this point in my life, I must say that nature takes its toll. All right, so maybe I don't have an economic struggle . . . which I had maybe thirty, forty years . . . so I have a nature struggle, past seventy.

There is something strange about nature that everything has to crumble. There's no material on earth, may it be steel or rock, that will stay that way forever. They all powder down in time. In the end everything on earth has to crumble. In the beginning there's a promise. The teeth get stronger, and the body gets stronger and then as it gets ready to function and it functions, it's destroyed and destroyed and destroyed. The human spirit—creation works in the opposite direction. In that place, you are creating, you are tapping life. But our physical life is mortal, so far as I'm concerned. Half the time we're growing up and there are labor pains right along the line, and half we're dying and that is the other pain.

But I'll tell you something, dear, that I've never feared death. To hell with it. I've met it daily and I want to feel that I was aware of it as possible. I think of Shankar, the great Indian dancer whom I sketched years ago . . . and of his father who was a great poet and used the symbol of the rose in his writings. He said that the world can be seen in one rose. And one rose can probably see the world. To have come to that essence of rose is a very high order of consciousness. In all its essences. And all the essences make one livingness. We know that Gertrude Stein is particularly known for the phrase "a rose is a rose is a rose." Every time I think of rose, the world is full of roses and the meaning of it. So I have come to these essences. To the place where it affirms my whole vision. And maybe you have to confront not being on earth to come to that place.

I do like to claim that my being here has shaken the earth a bit. Now I think language is so important and I think words . . . I think there are some words that can color your life, can kill you or make you a genius if you understand them. When I use the word *earth*, it's different than if I use the word *the universe*, or when I use the word *world*. The world—you think of it and it encompasses politics, it encompasses everything. But the earth—the earth includes the sun and the rain and all that. When you say the earth—you're down to the earth.

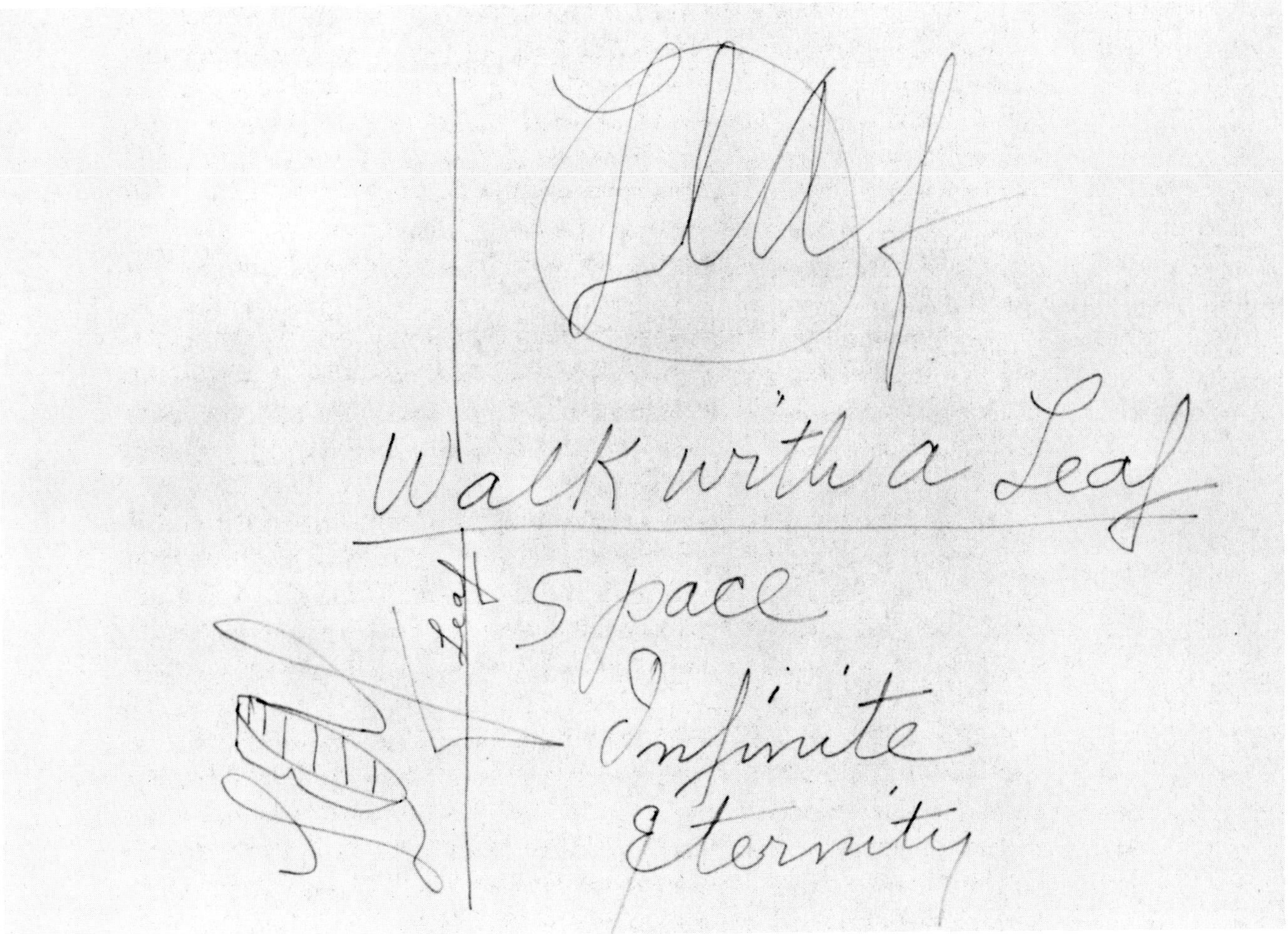

Walk with a Leaf

Space

Infinite
Eternity

Leaf

We can only live by the earth. We come from dust and earth. We feed on earth, even if it's distilled in some other form. And we go back to earth. And so there's something living in the *earth*. After a tree is cut down, it is assumed that the tree is dead. It may be the finish of that life as such. But even in that state of matter, there's activity, livingness. So there is no death in that sense. There's transformation. And the consciousness may be different. That's what we mean by "death"—the death of this consciousness. Well, I'm willing to accept that. Patterns of life change, but life doesn't change. Life is forever life. Livingness.

I have never feared not living, never, not even in youth. Because first, I found that life was difficult from the beginning until now. Second, I found the bridge somehow between the two worlds, which makes one, so I was never caught in it. We breathe air, don't we? But not far away, there's ether. Air and ether, the physical and the metaphysical.

I don't feel there's a period to this life. But I do not choose to think that I'm going to heaven or anything like that. In a way, that would offend me. And I don't want the idea that we have to come back. I feel that when I am finished—it's as if you make a vase. Well, you don't keep making that vase, you make it, and that's finished, and there's room for someone else to come and do something else.

You know, an interviewer had read somewhere that I had had a wonderful collection of American Indian pottery and quoted me as saying that if I were reincarnated, I would like to come back as an American Indian. Because I love everything American Indian. Their looks, their whole manner appeals to me. And so she asked me, at this point, how I felt about it. I don't believe in reincarnation but let's assume that I'll accept the question. She said, "What would you like to come back as in your next life?" I said, "Louise Nevelson" [laughs].

Louise Nevelson
2/22/76.

Bicentennial portrait of LN by Diana MacKown, 1976

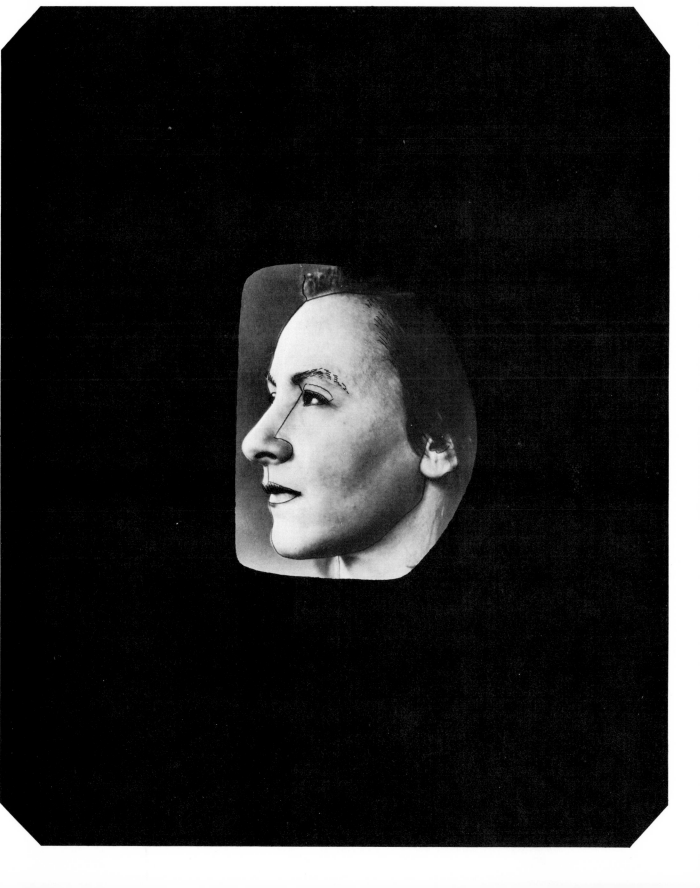

Mr. and Mrs. Charles Nevelson in the Peerless, Riverside Drive, 1922

LN, Rockland, Maine

LN, Rockland, Maine

Studio on 30th Street, 1950s

*LN, 30th Street,
with sculpture*

*LN, 30th Street
kitchen, with sculpture*

LN, 30th Street

Neith Nevelson, Florence, 1962

Maria and Elsbeth, New Fairfield, Connecticut, 1967

LN and Mike and family, Dorothy Miller far right, Christmas, 1974

Issa, LN's great-granddaughter, taken in Turkey, 1974

Nate Berliawsky, LN,
Skowhegan, Maine,
1973

Mike with Neith, Maria, and
Elsbeth, New Fairfield, Connecticut, 1966

LN in front of 29 Spring Street,
1966

LN and Marjorie Eaton, Palo Alto, California,
1972

LN at Newport, Rhode Island, 1970

LN being photographed by Patrick O'Higgins, 1967

Raggedy Ann with LN sculpture

View from roof of 29 Spring Street, New York City

View of lions on school building as seen from LN's roof

LN, dining room, 29 Spring Street, with Fat-Fat

LN on Mott Street in Chinatown, 1967

LN on 29 Spring Street roof , 1967

LN in front of wall in studio

Fat-Fat with sculpture

LN and Diana MacKown painting gold columns at Whitney retrospective

LN outside of Whitney during the retrospective, 1967

With Charles White at June Wayne's Tamarind, 1972

At Alphonso Ossorio's, Bridgehampton, Long Island, summer, 1970: with Jasper Johns, Marisol, Alphonso, Victoria Barr (and a Japanese photographer)

With Barbaralee Diamonstein, Long Island, 1974

LN and Gilbert Brownstone, 29 Spring Street

Picnic at Philip Johnson's estate, late 1960s

At Teeny Duchamp's, Villiers St. Grez, France, 1973

Diana MacKown and LN at Teeny Duchamp's, 1973

LN and John Cage, 1976

John Cage, LN, Merce Cunningham, 29 Spring Street

Living room, 29 Spring Street, 1974

LN, living room, 29 Spring Street, 1974

With Robert Indiana, Vinalhaven, Maine

LN, Bill Katz, Willy Eisenhart, Robert Creeley, 29 Spring Street, 1970s

At Creeley's, New Mexico, 1972

LN and Jean Dubuffet
Dining room, 29 Spring Street
Spring, 1974

Elsbeth and LN,
29 Spring Street, 1970

Neith, a visiting great dane, and Cous-Cous,
1965

Polar Bear

LN, 1975

Acknowledgments

To wonderful Louise Nevelson, for the hours and hours of taping over a period of many years—day and night—and for the great experience and joy in making this book a reality.

Special thanks to Annie Gottlieb, who worked hand in hand with me on the material, shaping and structuring it, for her great enthusiasm and understanding and the total fun of working with her.

In great appreciation to my editor, Patricia Cristol, whose depth and clarity of thought and perception set a perfect balance and tone for the book.

Thanks also to Arnold Glimcher, Pace Gallery; Helen Merrill; Richard Roberts, for access to the late Colette Roberts papers; Mrs. Jeremiah Russell; Anita Duquette of the Whitney Museum; and Garnett McCoy, the Archives of American Art. Thanks also to all members of Louise Nevelson's family for their cooperation, and to William Katz and William Eisenhart for their initial encouragement.

D.M.